Beginner's

SWEDISH

with 2 Audio CDs

HIPPOCRENE BEGINNER'S SERIES

ARABIC

ARMENIAN

ASSYRIAN

BASQUE

BULGARIAN (with 2 Audio CDs)

CHINESE (with 2 Audio CDs)

CZECH

DARI (with 1 Audio CD)

DUTCH

FINNISH

FRENCH

GAELIC

GREEK (with 2 Audio CDs)

HUNGARIAN

IRAQI ARABIC (with 2 Audio CDs)

IRISH (with 1 Audio CD)

ITALIAN

JAPANESE (with 2 Audio CDs)

KOREAN (with 2 Audio CDs)

LITHUANIAN

MAORI

NORWEGIAN (with 2 Audio CDs)

PERSIAN

POLISH (with 2 Audio CDs)

RUSSIAN

SERBO-CROATIAN

SHONA

SICILIAN

SLOVAK

SPANISH

TURKISH

UKRAINIAN

VIETNAMESE

WELSH

YORUBA (with 2 Audio CDs)

Also Available

INTERMEDIATE CHINESE (with 1 Audio CD)

MASTERING ARABIC (with 2 Audio CDs)

MASTERING POLISH (with 2 Audio CDs)

MASTERING SPANISH (with 2 Audio CDs)

Beginner's

SWEDISH

with 2 Audio CDs

SCOTT A. MELLOR

HIPPOCRENE BOOKS, INC.
New York

Text copyright © 2003, 2006 Scott A. Mellor.
Audio copyright © 2006 Scott A. Mellor.

1st paperback-with-audio edition, 2006.

ISBN 0-7818-1157-0

ISBN of previous edition: 0-7818-0951-7

Publisher: George Blagowidow
Book design and composition: Susan A. Ahlquist, Perfect Setting, East Hampton, NY
Book jacket and disc label design: Cynthia Mallard, Cynergie Studio, Raleigh, NC
Audio producers: Robert Stanley Martin, Scott A. Mellor
Audio speakers: Julie Berndt, Susan Brantly, Peppe Holmsten, Scott A. Mellor, Daniel Scheja
Recording engineer: Yaron Aldema
Audio recorded and mastered at World Music Connections/AM Studios, Inc., New York City

For more information, address:
HIPPOCRENE BOOKS, INC.
171 Madison Avenue
New York, NY 10016
www.hippocrenebooks.com

Cataloging-in-Publication Data available from the Library of Congress.

Printed in the United States of America.

*To Maud Lindqvist, who taught me Swedish,
and Susan Brantly, my constant inspiration.*

ACKNOWLEDGEMENTS

A book is seldom accomplished without the aid of others.

I would like to thank the Swedish Information Service and their fact sheets and information, which they give so readily. They were most helpful with the cultural information, especially the facts and figures. If anyone reading this book would like a great source of information regarding Sweden, I can highly recommend their website at www.swedenabroad.com/pages/start contacting them directly at:

Swedish Information Service
One Dag Hammarskjold Plaza
New York, N.Y. 10017-2201

Individuals meriting special thanks are Susan Brantly, Carina Karlsson, and Monica Wiklund who read through the manuscript and gave constant advice.

CONTENTS

INTRODUCTION

Swedish is the language spoken in Sweden and in parts of Finland. Linguistically Swedish is very similar to English, making it a relatively easy language to learn, though pronunciation can be problematic. The United States has strong cultural connections with Sweden including Swedish immigrants to the United States, imported products such as cars and telephones, and movie stars and producers. It is my hope that this book will make learning Swedish fun and interesting.

This book is designed to provide the English speaker with the basic grammar of Swedish and a general vocabulary of common words. Each lesson includes grammar points, a brief comparison of Swedish with English, and some important cultural information. The grammar rules are presented in a progressive order so that the most important grammar points are presented as early as possible without overwhelming the student. By the end of the book, the student should have a good understanding of all Swedish grammar.

Cultural information has been included so that the student will be able to understand significant events in Sweden. Sweden is rich in history and culture and, therefore, it is impossible to include everything. Care has been given to provide the student with as much information as possible so that the student will have some general knowledge when talking to Swedes about life, history, and lifestyle.

Finally, an etymology section has been included in which Swedish will be compared to English in the hopes of demonstrating that Swedish, although another language, is perhaps not completely foreign. I hope that this section will give students a sense of familiarity that will support their new command of Swedish.

ABBREVIATIONS

Parts of Speech and Other Grammatical Terms

adj.	adjective
adv.	adverb
art.	article
conj.	conjunction
com.	common gender
dir.	directional
intj.	interjection
inter.	interrogative
loc.	locational
n.	noun
neu.	neuter gender
pl.	plural
prep.	preposition
pro.	pronoun
ref.	reflexive
sing.	singular
v.	verb

GRAMMAR AT A GLANCE

1. The Swedish Alphabet

It is exceedingly difficult to acquire an accurate pronunciation of any foreign language solely through written instructions. However, the Swedish spelling system is relatively phonemic with a few exceptions that, once learned, make approximate pronunciation relatively easy. The accompanying audio CDs should help as well. Once one is familiar with the system, most Swedish texts can be read fairly comprehensibly. The basic alphabet consists of the 26 letters found in the English alphabet (though **c, q, w** and **z** are used mostly for foreign words) and three additional vowels in the following order:

a b c d e f g h i j k l m n o p q r s t u v w x y z å ä ö.

2. Vowels

The Swedish vowels, like the English, can be divided into two groups: front vowels formed in the front of your mouth and back vowels formed in the back of your mouth. The front vowels are: **e, i, y, ä**, and **ö**; and the back vowels are: **a, o, u**, and **å**. The pronunciation of these vowels depends on whether the vowel is long or short. Vowels in Swedish are either long or short depending on whether there is one or two consonants following (if there is one consonant they are long, e.g. **bus** *brat*; if there are two they are short, e.g. **buss** *bus*), giving them a different quality.

FRONT VOWELS

e   The long vowel resembles the English **e**ver, though longer:
                     skrev *wrote*; resa *to travel*; tre *three*
                     The short vowel resembles the English eff**e**ct:
                     ett *one/one* (*neu.*); exempel *example*; svenska *Swedish*

i   The long vowel resembles the English s**ee**:
bi *bee*; bil *car*; vi *we*
The short vowel resembles English **i**t:
innan *before*; till *to*; titta *to watch/look*

y   This is a sound not found in English. The long vowel resembles the German **ü** or the French **eu**. Form your mouth to say **u** and say **ee**, or just say **ee**:
fyra *four*; ny *new* (*com.*); by *town*
The short vowel, as with the long, is not found in English. It is a short version of the long. Say **i**t with slightly rounded lips:
lyssna *to listen*; nytt *new* (*neu.*); rygg *back*

ä   Like **e**, the long vowel resembles the English **e**ver:
väder *weather*; väg *road*; äta *eat*
The short vowel resembles English g**e**t:
bäst *best*; vägg *wall*; äpple *apple*

ö   The long vowel resembles the English work**er** with a less articulated **r** at the end:
snö *snow*; ö *island*; öga *eye*
The short vowel is the same as above, but shorter:
fönster *window*; höst *fall*; öppen *open* (*com.*)

In the pronunciation guide the vowels will be represented in the following manner:

a   long **aa**
short **ah**

e   long **ay**
short **eh**

i   long **ee**
short **i**

o   long **oo**
short **oh**

u	long **ew**
	short **u**
y	long **iw**
	short **i**
å	long **oa**
	short **oh**
ä	long **aeh**
	short **eh**
ö	long **er**
	short **ur**

BACK VOWELS

a
The long vowel resembles that of the English f**a**ther:
dag *day*, bra *good*, glas *glass*
The short vowel is shorter and lower and resembles the English c**a**t:
arm *arm*, ask *ash*, glass *ice cream*

o
The long vowel resembles the English ball**oo**n:
bok *book*, hon *she*, stol *chair*
The short vowel resembles the English h**o**pe:
blomma *flower*, klocka *clock*, ost *cheese*

u
The long vowel resembles the English f**ew**:
bus *cranky*, du *you* (*sing.*); nu *now*
The short vowel resembles the English p**u**t:
buss *bus*, full *full*, lunch *lunch*

å
The long vowel resembles the English h**oe**:
båt *boat*, skåp *cabinet*, två *two*
Like **o**, the short vowel resembles the English s**oa**p:
mått *measurement*, älder *age*, åtta *eight*

3. Consonants

The majority of consonants in Swedish are pronounced similarly to their English counterparts with a few exceptions.

c
: Sounds like **k** before **a, o, u, å**, and all consonants:
  café *café*; cancer *cancer*; och *and*
  Sounds like **s** before **e, i, y, ä**, and **ö**.
  cirka *cirka*; cello *cello*; centimeter *centimeter*

g
: Sounds like **g** before **a, o, u, å**, and all consonants:
  ganska *rather*; gråta *to cry*; gå *to go*
  Sounds like **y** before **e, i, y, ä**, and **ö**:
  ge *to give*; gäst *guest*; göra *to do*

j
: Sounds like **y**:
  familj *family*; ja *yes*; jord *earth*

k
: Sounds like **k** before **a, o, u, å**, and all consonants:
  kalla *to call*; ko *cow*; kål *cabbage*
  Sounds like **sh** before **e, i, y, ä**, and **ö**:
  kika *to look at*; kyrka *church*; köra *to drive*

l
: Though the learner of Swedish may find it easier to pronounce this sound the same as its English counterpart, the Swedish **l** is lighter than English, and more air escapes faster:
  laga *fix*; ligga *lie*; lång *long*

r
: Rolled, like the sound a motorcycle makes:
  radio *radio*; resa *to travel*; riva *to rip*

s
: Is always unvoiced as in the English **s**ix, and never voiced like the English i**s**:
  skrika *to scream*; skriva *to write*; stå *to stand*

v, w
: Sounds like **v**, the **w** is used mostly with foreign words:
  vad *what*; var *where*; vilken *which* (*com.*)

z   Sounds like **s**:
           zink *zink*; zon *zone*; zoolog *zoologist*

3.1 LETTER COMBINATIONS

There are a number of letter combinations that must be learned. These letter combinations may look impossible to pronounce on the surface, but they are really quite simple once the learner knows the sound the combinations make.

sj, skj, stj,   This sound is impossible to describe to the learner of the
sch, ch   language and even more difficult to pronounce (it is rather like a harsh **h**). There are Swedish dialects that pronounce it like the English **sh**, which is recommended.
           sju *seven*; skjuta *to shoot*; stjärna *star*

sk   Sounds like **sk** before **a, o, u**, and **å**:
           ska *will/shall*; sko *shoe*; skåp *cabinet*
           Again, it is recommended to pronounce this as the English **sh** before **e, i, y, ä**, and **ö**:
           skidor *skis*; skydd *protection* (*com.*); sköt *shot*

kj, tj   Sound like English **sh**:
           kjol *skirt*; tjära *tar*

hj, dj, lj, gj   Sound like **y**:
           hjälte *hero*; djur *animal*; ljus *light*; gjorde *did*

ng   Always sounds like the English si**ng**, and never like the English fi**ng**er:
           finger *finger*; lång *long*; många *many*

gn   Sounds like **ng-n**:
           regna *rain*; lugn *calm*; ugn *oven*

rd   Sounds like **d**, though your tongue is placed behind the ridge of your mouth:
           gjorde *did*; jord *earth*; mord *murder*

rg   Sounds like **ry**:
                      arg *angry*; borg *fortress*; Bergman *(a name)*

rl   Sounds like l, though your tongue is placed behind the
                      ridge of your mouth:
                      farlig *dangerous* (*com.*); karl *man*

rt   Sounds like t, though your tongue is placed behind the
                      ridge of your mouth:
                      parti *party (political)*; stort *big* (*neu.*)

rn   Sounds like n, though your tongue is placed behind the
                      ridge of your mouth:
                      barn *child*; kvarn *mill*; stjärna *star*

rs   Sounds like English **sh**, though your tongue is placed
                      behind the ridge of your mouth:
                      kors *cross*; person *person*; vars *whose*

3.2 EVERYDAY SPEECH

Often when a Swede is speaking in daily speech the final consonants are
left out.

dag (*day*)	Sounds like **da**
jag (*I*)	Sounds like **ya**
med (*with*)	Sounds like **me**
och (*and*)	Sounds like **o** or **ok**, never like English **och**
mig (*me*)	Sometimes spelled mej, sounds like **mey**
dig (*you sing.*)	Sometimes spelled dej, sounds like **dey**
sig (*he, she, it ref.*)	Sometimes spelled sej, sounds like **sey**
någon (*something/someone*)	Sometimes spelled nån, sounds like **non**
några	Sounds like **nora**
sådan	Sometimes spelled sån, sounds like **son**
sedan	Sometimes spelled sen, sounds like **sen**
de and dem	Sometimes spelled dom, sounds like **dom**

3.3 SPELLING

Many single syllable words in which the vowel is short have only a single *m* or *n*. However, the letters *m* and *n* are often doubled between two vowels.

kom *came, come!*	komma *to come*
rum *room*	rummet *the room*
man *man*	mannen *the man*
vän *friend*	vännen *the friend*

Further, a double m and n becomes single if another consonant is added:

sann *true (com.)*	sant *true (neu.)*
nummer *number*	numret *the number*

4. Length and Stress

Stress in Swedish, like English, is usually on the first syllable:

    fínger *finger*   résa *to travel*   númmer *number*

Usually when the stress is on a syllable other than the first syllable it is a borrowed word:

    polís *police*   cigarrétt *cigarette*   universitét *university*

5. Intonation and Word Melody

Swedish is a semi-tonal language, which means that there are some tones that give the language the sing-song reputation made popular by the Swedish chef on the Muppet Show, though in this show it is extremely exaggerated. Consider how in English an interrogative sentence goes up and a statement goes down in melody. It is much the same thing though within the word itself. A beginner will find it very difficult to hear and reproduce the tones, and it is recommended that the student not worry about it since it will, for the most part, inhibit comprehension. Thus tones are not shown in this book.

6. Verbs

A quick note about verbs in Swedish. Verbs in Swedish are very easy, even easier than English. There are four principle parts to the verb:

the infinitive: tala *to speak*   the present: talar *speaks*
the past: talade *spoke*   the perfect participle: talat *spoken*

Unlike English, all present tense forms in modern Swedish are the same. Thus the verb *to be* is conjugated:

jag **är** *I am*   vi **är** *we are*
du **är** *you* (*sing.*) *are*   ni **är** *you* (*pl.*) *are*
han/hon **är** *he/she is*   de (dom) **är** *they are*

Anyone who has tried a second language like Spanish, French or German will note how much easier Swedish is than those. There is one form not found in English called s-passive: talas *is spoken*. This last form usually does not present much of a problem for English speakers. There are no forms in Swedish like *is speaking* or *did speak*; these are handled with the simple present or past tense. More will be discussed about verbs in successive chapters.

7. Nouns

There are two genders in Swedish: *common* (*en* words) and *neuter* (*ett* words):

en flicka *a girl*   ett barn *a child*

Historically there were three genders. However, the masculine and feminine forms were merged into what is now the common gender. There is no useful way of telling whether a word is common or neuter. Though many more are common than neuter, they will simply have to be learned with the word.

Though not difficult, there is one oddity with nouns from an English speaker's point of view: the articles are suffixed onto the noun rather than a separate word as in English. Further, there are five common forms to the plurals, depending on whether the word is common or neuter. I have included a word as an example for each group as well as an approximate percentage of nouns in each group (based on the 1000 most common Swedish words from All-wood-Wilhelmsen's "Basic Word List"):

en flicka *a girl*	flickan *the girl*	
flickor *girls*	flickorna *the girls*	12%
en pojke *a boy*	pojken *the boy*	
pojkar *boys*	pojkarna *the boys*	37%
en cigarrett *a cigarette*	cigarretten *the cigarette*	
cigarretter *cigarettes*	cigarretterna *the cigarettes*	21%
ett äpple *an apple*	äpplet *the apple*	
äpplen *apples*	äpplena *the apples*	4%
ett barn *a child*	barnet *the child*	
barn *children*	barnen *the children*	26%

Though these plural ending may at first seem strange, English has similar endings though we no longer have gender. The English *-s* is similar to the Swedish *-r* plural ending for common nouns. Further, the neuter nouns are very similar to English: one deer-two deer, one sheep-two sheep and one ox-two oxen, one child-two children.

There are a few words that do not follow the above paradigms, but they are very few and they will be discussed in Lesson 1.

8. Adjectives

Briefly, adjectives are declined in much the same way the nouns are, i.e. there are differing forms depending on whether the noun is *common, neuter,* plural or definite:

en stor flicka *a big girl*	den stora flickan *the big girl*
två stora flickor *two big girls*	de stora flickorna *the big girls*

ett stort barn *a big child*	det stora barnet *the big child*
två stora barn *two big children*	de stora barnen *the big children*

Note that it is only the indefinite form that is different, e.g. en stor flicka/ett stort barn. This will be discussed in further detail in Lesson 3.

9. Word Order

Swedish is what is known as a verb-second language. This means the verb is always in the second position in a main clause. This is very similar to English except when an adverb or other part of the sentence is in the initial position:

> Johan åkte bil till affären idag. *Johan drove a car to the store today.*
> but: Idag åkte Johan bil till affären. *Today Johan drove a car to the store.*

Note that Johan has been moved past the verb in the second sentence. At first this may seem odd, but once again English has remnants of its verb-second roots. Consider a sentence like: *"What a nice day," said the man.* The end of this phrase, *said the man*, is also in verb-second word order. Ordinarily in English one would say *the man said*. This word order change in English is due to the fact that English once was, but is no longer, a verb-second language like Swedish. In short, any time a part of a sentence is in front of the subject and verb, the subject must follow the verb in a main clause.

This will be discussed further in Lesson 10.

LESSON
1

SAMTAL I

På flygplatsen.

Fru Lindquist, en affärskvinna som bor i Minneapolis, kommer till Arlanda flygplats i Stockholm för att träffa sin svenska affärskontakt:

FRU LINDQUIST: Ursäkta, var kan jag hämta mina väskor?

SAS PERSONAL: Följ de där människorna. Du måste genom
                    tullen. Ha passet redo.

FRU LINDQUIST: Tack.

I tullen visar fru Lindquist passet. Fru Lindquist har ingenting att förtulla och går snabbt igenom. På andra sidan går fru Lindquist till informationen och frågar kvinnan som står där var hon kan få tag på en taxi:

FRU LINDQUIST: God morgon, var kan jag få tag på en taxi?

INFORMATION: Precis utanför dörren borde det finnas en taxi.

FRU LINDQUIST: Tack.

Fru Lindquist hittar en taxi utan problem:

FRU LINDQUIST: Ursäkta mig, hur mycket kostar det att åka till
                    Stockholm?

TAXICHAUFFÖREN: Vart ska du?

FRU LINDQUIST: Till Hotell Kung Karl.

TAXICHAUFFÖREN: Det ligger i centrum. Det kostar ungefär sex
                    hundra kronor.

DIALOGUE I

At the airport.

Mrs. Lindquist, a businesswoman who lives in Minneapolis, arrives in Stockholm's Arlanda airport to meet with her Swedish business partner:

Ms. LINDQUIST: Excuse me, where do I go to claim my bags?

SCANDINAVIAN AIRLINES STAFF: Follow those people. You will also have to clear customs. Have your passport ready.

Ms. LINDQUIST: Thank you.

At immigration, Ms. Lindquist shows her passport. Ms. Lindquist has nothing to declare and passes quickly through. On the other side Ms. Lindquist goes to information and asks the woman standing there where she can find a taxi:

Ms. LINDQUIST: Good morning, where can I get a taxi?

INFORMATION: Just outside the door there should be a taxi.

Ms. LINDQUIST: Thank you.

Ms. Lindquist finds a taxi with no problem:

Ms. LINDQUIST: Excuse me, how much will it cost to go to Stockholm?

TAXI DRIVER: Where are you going?

Ms. LINDQUIST: Hotel Kung Karl.

TAXI DRIVER: That is in the center of town. It will cost about 600 crowns.

FRU LINDQUIST: Bra, hur lång tid tar det?

TAXICHAUFFÖREN: Det tar ungefär fyrtiofem minuter, det är cirka
                           femtio kilometer.

Fru Lindquist tackar och stiger in.

MS. LINDQUIST: Ok, how long will it take?

TAXI DRIVER: It takes about 45 minutes. It's about
                           50 kilometers.

Ms. Lindquist thanks him and gets in.

SAMTAL II

Det är Vinces första resa till Sverige. Han har precis kommit till Landvetter flygplats i Göteborg, och träffar en utbytesstudent som bodde hos honom förra året:

VINCE:	Här är mitt pass.
PASSKONTROLL:	Du talar svenska! Hur länge stannar du i Sverige?
VINCE:	Ungefär tre veckor.
PASSKONTROLL:	Orsak till besök?
VINCE:	Jag är här på semester.
PASSKONTROLL:	Var ska du bo?
VINCE:	Hos en kompis.
PASSKONTROLL:	Bra, här får du passet. Välkommen till Sverige.
VINCE:	Tack, var ligger närmaste växelkontor?
PASSKONTROLL:	Precis på andra sidan av dörren.
VINCE:	Tack.

När Vince har gått genom tullen går han till växelkontoret:

VINCE:	Jag skulle vilja växla tre hundra dollar tack. Jag har resecheckar.
VÄXELPERSONAL:	Du får tretusenetthundrasjuttioen kronor.

DIALOGUE II

This is Vince's first trip to Sweden. He has just arrived at Gothenburg's Land-vetter airport and is meeting an exchange student that stayed with him last year:

VINCE: Here is my passport.

PASSPORT CONTROL: You speak Swedish! How long are you staying in Sweden?

VINCE: About three weeks.

PASSPORT CONTROL: Reason for the visit?

VINCE: I'm here on vacation.

PASSPORT CONTROL: Where will you be staying?

VINCE: At a friend's.

PASSPORT CONTROL: Ok, here is your passport. Welcome to Sweden.

VINCE: Thanks, where is the nearest exchange office?

PASSPORT CONTROL: Just on the other side of the door.

VINCE: Thanks

After Vince has gone through customs he goes to the exchange office:

VINCE: I would like to exchange 300 dollars please. I have traveler's checks.

EXCHANGE OFFICER: You get 3171 crowns.

VINCE:	Tack. Hur kommer jag till centrum?
VÄXELPERSONAL:	Du kan ta taxi, men det är mycket dyrt. Det finns bussar som tar ungefär tjugo minuter och kostar femtio kronor.
VINCE:	Var står bussen till stan?
VÄXELPERSONAL:	Precis utanför dörren där.
VINCE:	Tack.

VINCE: Thanks. How can I get downtown?

EXCHANGE OFFICER: You can take a taxi, but it is very expensive. There are
                              buses that take about 20 minutes and cost 50 crowns.

VINCE: Where is the bus into town?

EXCHANGE OFFICER: Just out the door, there.

VINCE: Thanks.

VOCABULARY

affärskontakt 3 *n. com.*	ahff**ehr**skohnt**ah**kt	business contact
affärskvinna 1 *n. com.*	ahff**ehr**shk**v**innah	businesswoman
andra *adj.*	**ah**ndrah	another
Arlanda	**ah**rlahndah	Stockholm airport
att (*inf.* particle)	ahtt	to
av *prep.*	aav	by
besök 5 *n. neu.*	behs**erk**	visit
bo III *v.*	boo	live
borde *v.*	**bo**hrdeh	should
bra *adj. adv.*	braa	good
buss 2 *n. com.*	buss	bus
centrum *n. neu.*	s**eh**ntrum	downtown
chauffför 3 *n. com.*	shohff**err**	chauffeur
de *pron.*	dohm	they
det *neu.*	day	it
det finns	deh finns	there is/are
dollar	**do**hllahr	dollar
du *sing.*	dew	you
dyrt *adj. neu.*	diwrt	expensive
där *adv.*	daehr	there (location)
dörr 2 *n. com.*	derrr	door
efter *prep.*	**eh**ftehr	after
en *com.*	ehn	one/a
femtio	f**eh**mtee	fifty
finnas IV i-a-u *v.*	f**i**nnahs	exist
flygplats 3 *n. com.*	fl**iw**gplahts	airport
fru 2 *n. com.*	frew	Mrs./Ms./wife
fråga I *v.*	fr**ao**ga	ask
fyrtiofem	f**iw**rteefehm	forty-five
få (får-fick-fått) *v.*	fao (fehk-fohtt)	get
följa IIa *v.*	f**er**lyah	follow
förra *adv.*	f**err**ah	before/previous
första	f**err**shta	first
förtulla *v.*	ferrt**u**llah	declare

Swedish	Pronunciation	English
genom *prep.*	yehnohm	through
god *adj.*	goo	good
gå V (gå-gick-gått) *v.*	gao (yik-gohtt)	walk
Göteborg	yertehbohry	Gothenburg
ha V (har-hade-haft) *v.*	haa	have
han *pro.*	hahn	he
hitta I *v.*	hitah	find
hon *pro.*	hoon	she
hos *prep.*	hoos	at (at someone's house)
hotell 5 *n. neu.*	hohtehll	hotel
hundra 5	hundrah	hundred
hur *inter.*	hewr	how
hämta I *v.*	hehmtah	fetch
här *adv. loc.*	hehr	here
i *prep.*	ee	in
igenom *prep.*	eeyehnohm	in through
information 3 *n. com.*	infohrmaashoon	information
ingenting *n. neu.*	ingehnting	nothing
jag *pro.*	yaag	I
kan V *v.*	kahn	can
kilometer *n. neu.*	keelohmaytehr *or* sheeohmaytehr	kilometer
komma IV o-o-o *v.*	kohmmah	come
kompis 2 *n. com.*	kohmpees	friend
kosta I *v.*	kohstah	cost
krona 1 *n. com.*	kroonah	crown
kung 2 *n. com.*	kung	king
kvinna 1 *n. com.*	kvinnah	woman
Landvetter	lahndvehtterr	Gothenburg airport
ligga (ligger-låg-legat) *v.*	liggah	lie
långt *adj.*	lohngkt	long
länge *adv.*	lehngeh	long (time)
med *prep.*	may	with
men *conj.*	mehn	but
mig *pro.*	may	me
mina *pro. com. pl.*	meenah	my
minut 3 *n. com.*	minewt	minute
mitt *pro. neu.*	mitt	my

morgon (*pl.* morgnar) *n. com.*	**mohr**rohn	morning
mycket *adv.*	**mi**wkeh	much
måste *v.*	**moh**steh	must
människa 1 *n. com.*	**meh**nnishah	person (*pl.* people)
närmaste *adj.*	**mehr**mahsteh	nearest
och *conj.*	oh *or* ohk	and
orsak 3 *n. com.*	**ohr**shaak	reason
pass 5 *n. neu.*	pahss	passport
passkontroll 3 *n. com.*	pahsskohtr**ohl**l	passport control
personal 3 *n. com.*	pehrshohn**ahl**	personnel
precis *adv.*	preh**sees**	exactly
problem 5 *n. neu.*	prohbl**ehm**	problem
på *prep.*	poa	on
redo *adj.*	**ray**doa	ready
resa IIb *v.*	**ray**sah	travel
resecheckar 2 *n. com.*	**ray**sehshehkkahr	traveler's checks
semester 2 *n. com.*	sehm**eh**stehr	vacation
sex	**seh**ks	six
sida 1 *n. com.*	**see**dah	side
sig *pro.*	say	himself/herself
sin *pro. com.*	seen	his own/her own
ska *v.*	skaa	will
skulle *v.*	sk**u**lleh	would
snabbt *adv.*	snahbt	quickly
som *pro.*	sohm	who/which/that
stad 3 *n. com.*	staad	city
stan	staan	the city
stanna I *v.*	st**ah**nnah	stay
stiga IV i-e-i *v.*	st**ee**gah	get in
stå III *v.*	stoa	stand
svenska *n.*	sv**eh**nskah	Swedish (language)
Sverige *n. com.*	sv**eh**reeyeh	Sweden
ta V (tar-tog-tagit) *v.*	taa	take
tack	tahkk	thanks
tag 5 *n. neu.*	taag	ahold
tala I *v.*	t**aa**lah	speak
taxi (*pl.* taxi) *n. com.*	t**ah**ksee	taxi

till *prep.*	till	to
tjugo	sh**oo**goa	twenty
tre	tray	three
träffa I *v.*	tr**eh**ffah	meet
tull 2 *n. com.*	tull	customs
ungefär *adv.*	unyeh**fehr**	about/approximately
ursäkta I *v.*	ewr**sheh**ktah	excuse
utan *conj.*	**ew**tahn	without
utanför *adv.*	**ew**tahn**ferr**	outside
utbytesstudent 3 *n. com.*	ewtbiwtehsstewd**ehn**t	exchange student
var *v.*	vaar	was
var *adv.*	vaar	where
vara *v.*	v**aa**rah	be
vart *adv. dir.*	vahrt	where to
vecka 1 *n. com.*	v**eh**kkah	week
vilja (vill-ville-velat) *v.*	vilyah	want
visa I *v.*	v**ee**sah	show
välkommen *adj.*	vaelk**oh**mmehn	welcome
väska 1 *n. com.*	v**eh**skah	suitcase/bag
växelkontor 5 *n. com.*	v**eh**ksehlkohnt**oor**	exchange office
växelpersonal *n. com.*	v**eh**ksehlpehrshohn**ahl**	exchange personnel
växla I *v.*	v**eh**kslah	exchange
åka IIb *v.*	**ao**kah	go (by vehicle)
år 5 *n. neu.*	ohr	year
är *v.*	ehr	am/is/are

USEFUL EXPRESSIONS

Här är mitt pass.	Here is my passport.
Jag är här i affärer.	I am here on business.
Jag är här på semester.	I am here on vacation.
Jag stannar en vecka.	I am staying a week.
Jag har ingenting att förtulla.	I have nothing to declare.
Talar du engelska?	Do you speak English?

COUNTRIES

Australien	Australia
Belgien	Belgium
Danmark	Denmark
Finland	Finland
Frankrike	France
Grekland	Greece
Irland	Ireland
Island	Iceland
Israel	Israel
Italien	Italy
Japan	Japan
Kanada	Canada
Kina	China
Mexico	Mexico
Nederländerna	Netherlands
Norge	Norway
Polen	Poland
Portugal	Portugal
Ryssland	Russia
Schweiz	Switzerland
Spanien	Spain
Storbritannien	Great Britain
Sverige	Sweden
Tjeckiska republiken	Czech Republic
Turkiet	Turkey

Tyskland   Germany
USA   USA
Österrike   Austria

LANGUAGES

danska   Danish
engelska   English
finska   Finnish
flamländska   Flemish
franska   French
grekista   Greek
hebreiska   Hebrew
holländska   Dutch
irska   Irish
isländska   Icelandic
italienska   Italian
japanska   Japanese
kinesiska   Chinese
norska   Norwegian
polska   Polish
portugisiska   Portuguese
ryska   Russian
spanska   Spanish
svenska   Swedish
tjeckista   Czech
turkiska   Turkish
tyska   German

GRAMMAR

1.   Pronouns

1.1   SUBJECT PRONOUNS

In Swedish, the pronouns that are used as the subjects of sentences are as follows:

jag	I
du	you *sing.*
hon	she
han	he
den	it *com.*
det	it *neu.*
vi	we
ni	you *pl.*
de (dohm)	they

1.2   OBJECT PRONOUNS

In Swedish, the pronouns that are used as the objects of sentences are as follows:

mig (mey)	me
dig (dey)	you *sing.*
henne	her
honom	him
den	it *com.*
det	it *neu.*
oss	us
er	you *pl.*
dem (dohm)	them

Note:
Please note that Swedish has a second person plural. However, unlike other languages like French and German, it is no longer used as a formal form (like

the German *Sie*, the French *vous*, or the Spanish *vosotros*). Also note that *de*, *dem*, *mig*, and *dig* are not pronounced as they are spelled. The pronunciation is included in parentheses.

2.   Nouns

2.1 GENDER

The Swedish language has two genders: common (*en* words) and neuter (*ett* words). Common is made up of historical masculine and feminine genders that collapsed into a single gender. Roughly two thirds of the words are common, and the remaining third is neuter. Swedish gender is not a logical category and is not determined by the word ending as in other languages and, therefore, it must be learned with the word. Words with almost identical meaning can have different genders:

en villa *a house*   ett hus *a house/building*
en båt *a boat*   ett skepp *a ship*

2.2 PLURALS

There are five basic endings for plurals in Swedish, two for neuter (*ett*) nouns and three for common (*en*) nouns. The rules for *ett* nouns are relatively easy: if the noun ends in a consonant there is no ending; if it ends in a vowel the ending is *-n*. Plurals for common nouns are slightly more complicated: if the noun ends in an *-a* the plural is *-or*. There are two more plural endings for nouns, the rules for which are too complicated to be of any value, therefore it is best to memorize them.

1. en flicka *a girl*   flick**or** *girls*
2. en pojke *a boy*   pojk**ar** *boys*
3. en cigarett *a cigarette*   cigarett**er** *cigarettes*
4. ett äpple *an apple*   äppl**en** *apples*
5. ett barn *a child*   barn *children*

There are a few slight modifications to these plural rules. They often involve the liquids *r* and *l*, and the nasal *n*.

Nouns ending in -el, -en, and -er drop the final e before the plural ending.

en toffel *a slipper*	två toffl**or** *two slippers*
en nyckel *a key*	två nyckl**ar** *two keys*
en syster *a sister*	två systr**ar** *two sisters*
en sägen *a legend*	två sägn**er** *two legends*
en regel *a rule*	två regl**ar** *two rules*

Nouns ending in -on and -ar drop the final vowel before the plural ending.

en afton *an evening*	två aftn**ar** *two evenings*
en morgon *a morning*	två morgn**ar** *two mornings*
en sommar *a summer*	två somr**ar** *two summers*

There is a small group of nouns that end in a vowel and only take an -r ending in the plural.

en ko *a cow*	två ko**r** *two cows*
en sko *a shoe*	två sko**r** *two shoes*

There is a small group of words that change the stem vowel in the plural. What follows is not an exhaustive list, but contains the most common words. English has this plural form too, though it is a smaller group, e.g. one tooth, two teeth, one foot, two feet.

en and *a duck*	två änder *two ducks*
en bokstav *a letter (alphabet)*	två bokstäver *two letters*
en brand *a fire*	två bränder *two fires*
en hand *a hand*	två händer *two hands*
ett land *a country*	två länder *two countries*
en natt *a night*	två nätter *two nights*
en rand *a strip*	två ränder *two strips*
en stad *a city*	två städer *two cities*
en tand *a tooth*	två tänder *two teeth*
en stång *a pole*	två stänger *two poles*
en tång *a tong*	två tänger *two tongs*

en ledamot *a member*	två ledamöter *two members*
en son *a son*	två söner *two sons*
en bok *a book*	två böcker *two books*
en fot *a foot*	två fötter *two feet*
en rot *a root*	två rötter *two roots*

Notice that the above group contains both neuter and common nouns. There are also a few words that are irregular.

en man *a man*	två män *two men*
ett öga *an eye*	två ögon *two eyes*
ett öra *an ear*	två öron *two ears*

There is also a very active group ending in *-are*, equivalent to English *-er*, that is the same in the indefinite singular and plural:

en arbetare *one worker*	två arbetare *two workers*
arbetaren *the worker*	arbetarna *the workers*

Ultimately it is important for the learner of Swedish to memorize the plural forms with the word.

2.3 DEFINITENESS

Unlike English, the Swedish definite article is not a separate word but a suffix.

flickan *the girl*	flickorna *the girls*
pojken *the boy*	pojkarna *the boys*
cigarretten *the cigarette*	cigarretterna *cigarettes*
äpplet *the apple*	äpplena *the apples*
barnet *the child*	barnen *the children*

Note that the *e* in *en* or *ett* is dropped when the noun ends in a vowel.

3. Making a Sentence Negative

The word *inte* negates a sentence. It follows the verb in a normal main clause. Unlike English there is no additional modal, like the English *do*, in the sentence.

Jag dricker.
I drink/am drinking.
Jag äter.
I eat/am eating.
Jag talar svenska
I speak Swedish.

Jag dricker inte.
I do not drink/ I am not drinking.
Jag äter inte.
I do not eat/I am not eating.
Jag talar inte svenska.
I do not speak Swedish.

4. Making a Sentence a Question

Swedish does not use, as English does, an emphatic with the verb *do* to form its questions. Rather, Swedish merely inverts the word order, placing the verb first.

Du dricker.
You drink.
Du äter.
You eat.
Du talar svenska.
You speak Swedish.

Dricker du?
Do you drink?
Äter du?
Do you eat?
Talar du svenska?
Do you speak Swedish?

ÖVNINGAR

(Exercises)

I.   Skriv följande på svenska (Write the following in Swedish).

1. I	5. she	9. me
2. them	6. her	10. they
3. we	7. you *obj. sing.*	11. him
4. us	8. you *sub. pl.*	12. he

II. Vilket genus är de följande substantiven (Which gender are the following nouns)?

1. affärskvinna	6. hotell
2. besök	7. kompis
3. dörr	8. flygplats
4. fru	9. vecka
5. kvinna	10. minut

III. Skriv de följande substantiven i pluralis (Write the following nouns into plurals).

1. människa	6. morgon
2. pass	7. kompis
3. chaufför	8. problem
4. fru	9. vecka
5. utbytesstudent	10. sida

IV. Skriv de följande substantiven i bestämd form (Write the following nouns in the definite form).

1. väska	6. hotell
2. dagar	7. kompisar
3. kungar	8. år
4. fru	9. vecka
5. pass	10. krona

V. Skriv de följande meningar i negativ form (Write the following sentences in a negative form).

   1. Jag talar svenska.
   2. Han har passet.
   3. Jag är här på semester.
   4. Du kan få tag på en taxi där.
   5. Hon är en affärskvinna.

VI. Skriv de följande som frågor (Write the following as questions).

   1. Du talar svenska.
   2. Han har passet.
   3. Han är här på semester.
   4. Jag kan få tag på en taxi där.
   5. Hon är en affärskvinna.

ETYMOLOGY

Swedish and English are both Germanic languages, though distant cousins. This means that there are many words that are related in both languages. The word etymology comes from the Greek words *etmos* (true or real) and *logos* (word or account). Etymology traces the derivation of words and shows their meaning and relationship with words in other languages. It is sometimes helpful to understand the relationship a Swedish word has with an English one, especially when trying to remember the Swedish meaning. The reader will note several words that are very similar to their English counterparts in the lesson above.

dricka	drink
tack	thank
god	good
natt	night
kommer	comes
dag	day

However, beware the false cognate, i.e. words that appear the same but have quite different meanings. The Swedish *vill* may look like the English *will* but it means *want*.

The words above started as the same over a thousand years ago, but changed during that time. Notice that in Swedish, the letter *n* disappeared when before the *k* sound, so the Swedish *dricka* and *tack* are the English *drink* and *thank*. In English, the final *g* sound became a *y*, so there is now Swedish *dag* and English *day*.

Swedish plural endings may seem strange to the English speaker, but both systems have a common ancestor, and remnants of these endings can be found in English. The original plural ending in the Germanic languages became an -*s* in English and an -*r* in Swedish. The change in stem vowels is also found in English, e.g. one foot, two feet, one tooth, two teeth. Even the -*n* plural in the Swedish neuter is found in English: one ox, two oxen.

Geography

Sweden, with a population of about nine million, has a relatively small population in a large area. The majority of the population lives in the southernmost third of the country. Sweden is one of the countries furthest from the equator and is found at roughly the same latitude as Alaska. It is for this reason that Sweden is sometimes known as the land of the midnight sun. In the summer the sun only sets for a few hours in Stockholm and not at all in the city of Kiruna. However, in the winter the sun comes up for only a few hours in Stockholm and not at all in Kiruna. In size, Sweden is a little larger than California.

The landscape of Sweden is varied, with mountains in the north and plains and rocky areas in the south. The southernmost part of Sweden, called Skåne with Malmö as its capital, is fertile plains. To the north is a heavily wooded highland region called Norrland. Between the cities of Stockholm and Gothenburg, the landscape is primarily rock with a varied terrain of fields, hills, and lakes. The northern region comprising the northern three-fifths of Sweden is called Norrland. Kiruna is known to be one of the largest cities in the world in square miles, though very sparsely populated with only about 26,000 inhabitants. The terrain of this region consists of a rolling landscape with hills and mountains, forests, and large river valleys. To the west lies Norway. Along the border runs a mountain range with peaks rising from 3,000 to 7,000 feet above sea level. The lower parts of the mountain range are heavily forested.

Despite Sweden's northern location it enjoys a relatively mild climate due to its proximity to the Atlantic, with its warm Gulf Stream. The weather is variable with rain followed by beautiful sunshine in only a few hours. Fall and winter arrive early, but are not as harsh as in places in the United States such as Minnesota or the Dakotas. Norrland, understandably, has colder and longer winters than Stockholm or Gothenburg.

The total area of Sweden is 173,731 sq.miles. The distance north to south is 977 miles and from east to west is 310 miles. It is 301 miles from Stockholm to Gothenburg, 276 from Gothenburg to Malmö and 385 from Malmö to Stockholm. The population of Stockholm is approximately 1.6 million and about 790,000 live in Gothenburg, whereas only a half million live in Malmö.

LESSON
2

SAMTAL I

Hälsningar och presentationer.

Fru Lindquist checkar in på hotellet:

FRU LINDQUIST: God morgon. Jag har bokat ett rum. Mitt namn är Lindquist.

RECEPTION: Ja visst fru Lindquist. Du har rum nummer 207. Vill du ha hjälp med dina väskor?

FRU LINDQUIST: Ja, tack.

När hon har checkat in hälsar en man henne vid receptionen:

HERR ANDERSSON: Hej, är du fru Lindquist?

FRU LINDQUIST: Ja, jag heter fru Lindquist.

HERR ANDERSSON: Jag heter Andersson. Trevligt att träffas. Jag ville träffa dig på flygplatsen, men jag var försenad.

FRU LINDQUIST: Det är bra, jag tog taxi hit. Min dygnsrytm är lite rubbad. Jag tänkte jag skulle sova middag.

HERR ANDERSSON: Bra. Sov middag. Om du vill kan jag komma tillbaka i kväll och vi kan gå ut på restaurang och äta middag.

FRU LINDQUIST: Det låter trevligt. Går klockan sex bra?

HERR ANDERSSON: Klockan sex är fint. Vi ses då.

DIALOGUE I

Greetings and introductions.

Mrs Lindquist checks into the hotel:

Ms. LINDQUIST: Good morning. I have reserved a room. My name is Ms. Lindquist.

RECEPTION: Of course, Ms. Lindquist. You are in room 207. Would you like help with your bags?

Ms. LINDQUIST: Yes, thank you.

After checking in a man greets her at the reception:

MR. ANDERSSON: Hello, are you Ms. Lindquist?

Ms. LINDQUIST: Yes, my name is Ms. Lindquist.

MR. ANDERSSON: I am Mr. Andersson. Pleased to meet you. I wanted to meet you at the airport, but I was delayed.

Ms. LINDQUIST: That's ok, I took a taxi here. I am a little jet-lagged. I thought I would take a nap.

MR. ANDERSSON: Good. You take a nap and if you like I can come back this evening and we can go out to a restaurant and have dinner.

Ms. LINDQUIST: That sounds very nice. How about six o'clock?

MR. ANDERSSON: Six o'clock is fine. I will see you then.

SAMTAL II

Vince kommer till Göteborgs centrum till ett ställe som heter Nordstan, en galleria. Han frågar efter en telefon:

VINCE: Ursäkta mig, var finns det en telefon?

MAN: Där borta, i hörnet.

VINCE: Tack.

Vince går till telefonen och ringer sin kompis som heter Eva.

VINCE: Hallå, kan jag få tala med Eva?

EVA: Det är Eva. Är det du Vince?

VINCE: Ja, jag är här i Göteborg, på ett ställe som heter Nordstan.

EVA: Kul. Stanna där, jag kommer och hämtar dig. Ta en kopp kaffe på kaféet där.

VINCE: Okej, vi ses snart. Hej då.

DIALOGUE II

Vince arrives in downtown Gothenburg at a place called Nordstan, a shopping mall. He asks to find a telephone:

VINCE: Excuse me, where can I find a telephone?

MAN: Over there, in the corner.

VINCE: Thanks.

Vince goes to the telephone and calls his friend, whose name is Eva.

VINCE: Hello, may I speak with Eva?

EVA: This is Eva. Is that you, Vince?

VINCE: Yes, I am here in Gothenburg, at a place called Nordstan.

EVA: Cool. Stay there and I will come and get you. Get a cup of coffee at the coffee shop there.

VINCE: Ok, I will see you soon. Bye.

VOCABULARY

boka I *v.*	bookah	book/reserve
borta *adv.*	bohrtah	away
checka in *v.*	shehkkah in	check in
dina *pro. sing. pl.*	deennah	your
dygnsrytm 3 *n. com.*	dingnsritm	jet lag
galleria 1 *n. com.*	gahllehreeah	shopping mall
fint *adv.*	fint	fine
försenad *adj.*	ferrshehnaad	late
hallå *intj.*	hahlloa	hello
hej då *intj.*	hay dao	good-bye
henne *pro.*	hehnneh	her
hit *adv. dir.*	heet	here
hjälp 4 *n. neu.*	yehlp	help
hälsa I *v.*	hehlsah	greet
hörn 5 *n. neu.*	herrn	corner
in *adv.*	in	inside
ja *intj.*	jaa	yes
kafé (*pl.* kaféer) *n. neu.*	kaafay	café
kaffe *n. neu.*	kahffeh	coffee
klocka 1 *n. com.*	klohkkah	clock
kopp 2 *n com.*	kohpp	cup
kul (undeclineable, slang) *adj.*	kewl	cool/fun
kväll 2 *n. com.*	kvehll	evening
lite *adv.*	leeteh	a little
låta IV å-ä-å *v.*	loatah	sound
man *pro.*	mahn	one/man/husband
middag 2 *n. com.*	middah	afternoon
min *pro.*	min	mine/my
namn 5 *n. neu.*	nahmn	name
Nordstan	nohrdstahn	name of mall
nummer 5 *n. neu.*	nummehr	number
okej *intj.*	ohkay	ok
om *conj.*	ohm	if

reception 3 *n. com.*	rehsehpsh**oo**n	reception
restaurang 3 *n. com.*	reste**rah**ng	restaurant
ringa IIa *v.*	ringah	call
rubbad *adj.*	**ru**bbahd	upset/dislodged
rum 5 *neu.*	rum	room *n.*
ses *v.*	says	see each other *or*
		be seen
snart *adv.*	snahrt	soon
sova middag *v.*	s**oh**vah m**i**dah	take a nap
sova IV o-o-o *v.*	s**oh**vah	sleep
stanna I *v.*	sta**h**nnah	stay
ställe 4 *n. neu.*	ste**h**lleh	place
telefon 3 *n. com.*	tehleh**foh**n	telephone
tillbaka *adv.*	till**baa**kah	back
trevligt *adv.*	tr**eh**vlit	pleasant
träffas *v.*	tr**eh**ffahs	meet each other *or*
		be met
tänka IIb *v.*	t**eh**nkah	to think
upp *adv. dir.*	upp	up
ut *adv. dir.*	ewt	out
vid *prep.*	veed	at
visst *adj.*	visst	course/certain
äta IV ä-å-ä *v.*	**ae**htah	eat

USEFUL EXPRESSIONS

God morgon.	Good morning.
God dag.	Good day.
God afton.	Good evening.
God natt.	Good night.
Hej.	Hi.
Hej då.	Good-bye.
Ja.	Yes.
Nej.	No.
Tack.	Thank you.
Varsågod.	You are welcome./Here you are.
Hur står det till?	How are you?
Hur är läget? (slang/informal)	How are you?
Vad heter du?	What is your name?
Jag heter _____.	My name is_____.
Trevligt att träffas.	Nice to meet you.
Jag har beställt rum.	I have reserved a room.
Jag ringde från flygplatsen.	I called from the airport.
Jag skulle vilja ha ett rum.	I would like a room.
... en svit.	... a suite.

Vad är det för väder idag?	What kind of weather is it today?
Det är bra väder.	It is nice weather.
Det är varmt.	It is warm.
Det är kallt.	It is cold.
Det regnar.	It is raining.
Solen skiner.	The sun is shining.
Det blåser.	It is windy.
Det snöar.	It is snowing.

GRAMMAR

1. Verbs

1.1 WEAK VERBS

There are only four principle parts to the verb in Swedish, not including the two participles that will be discussed in Lesson 9. Verbs are found primarily in two classes: weak verbs and strong verbs. For weak verbs the tenses are formed by adding the following to the imperative or command form: the infinitive *-a*, the present tense *-r*, the past tense *-de*, and the perfect tense *-t*. There are three types of weak verbs that will be labeled I, II, and III in this book:

I
arbeta! *work!*
att arbeta *to work*   arbetar *work/works*
arbetade *worked*   (har/hade) arbetat *(have/had) worked*

Note that the *-a* is not doubled for the infinitive form.

Group II can be broken into two groups, those that end in a voiced consonant and those ending in a voiceless consonant.

IIa
behöv! *need!*
att behöva *to need*   behöver *need/needs*
behövde *needed*   (har/hade) behövt *(have/had) needed*

IIb
läs! *read!*
att läsa *to read*   läser *read/reads*
läste *read*   (har/hade) läst *(have/had) read*

Class III is marked by the absence of an -a in the infinitive form, the doubling of the past d and perfect t, and they end in a vowel in the command form. It is a relatively small group with only about a dozen verbs:

III
tro! *believe!*
att tro *to believe*   tror *believe/believes*
trodde *believed*   (har/hade) trott *(have/had) believed*

1.2 STRONG VERBS

The fourth class of verbs are strong verbs and they vary widely. Here are rules for the formation of strong verbs, but the rules are often more difficult to remember than memorizing the verb forms. The letter changes will be included in the vocabulary and dictionary entries at the back of the book. Below are a few examples that will help the student understand the paradigm:

IV i-e-i
skriv! *write!*
att skriva *to write*   skriver *write/writes*
skrev *wrote*   (har/hade) skrivit *(have/had written)*

IV i-a-u
bind! *bind!*
att binda *to bind*   binder *bind/binds*
band *bound*   (har/hade) bundit *(have/had) bound*

Note that the examples given are in English strong verbs themselves.

1.3 IRREGULAR VERBS

Like every other language, Swedish has a number of irregular verbs. They are also often the most common verbs. Below are a few of the more common irregular verbs:

V
var! *be!*
att vara *to be*   är *am/are/is*
var *was/were*   (har/hade) varit *(have/had) been*

V
ha! *have!*
att ha *to have*   har *has/have*
hade *had*   (har/hade) haft *(have/had) had*

V
ge! *give!*
att ge *to give*   ger *gives*
gav *gave*   (har/hade) gett *(have/had) given*

1.4 FUTURE, CONDITIONAL AND VERBAL COMBINATIONS

There is no future tense. As in English, the future is expressed with a separate word, **ska** *will*, and the infinitive without its marker:

jag ska arbeta *I will work*
du ska behöva *you (sing.) will need*
han ska läsa *he will read*
hon ska tro *she will believe*
ni ska skriva *you (pl.) will write*
de ska binda *they will bind*

Another, perhaps more common way to express the future is by using **kommer att** *going to*:

jag kommer att arbeta *I am going to work*
du kommer att behöva *you (sing.) are going to need*
han kommer att läsa *he is going to read*
hon kommer att tro *she is going to believe*
ni kommer att skriva *you (pl.) are going to write*
de kommer att binda *they are going to bind*

A third way to express the future is to use the present with an adverbial:

jag arbetar imorgon *I work tomorrow*
du behöver imorgon *you (sing.) need tomorrow*
han läser imorgon *he reads tomorrow*
hon tror imorgon *she believes tomorrow*

ni skriver imorgon *you (pl.) write tomorrow*
de binder imorgon *they bind tomorrow*

Conditionals are formed much the same way as future, with the past of **ska**, namely **skulle**:

jag skulle arbeta *I would work*
du skulle behöva *you (sing.) would need*
han skulle läsa *he would read*
hon skulle tro *she would believe*
ni skulle skriva *you (pl.) would write*
de skulle binda *they would bind*

Finally there is the conditional perfect:

jag skulle ha arbetat *I would have worked*
du skulle ha behövt *you (sing.) would have needed*
han skulle ha läst *he would have read*
hon skulle ha trott *she would have believed*
ni skulle ha skrivit *you (pl.) would have written*
de skulle ha bundit *they would have bound*

1.5   PASSIVE VERBS

This final tense is the passive tense, which is formed with an -s:

det behövs av mig *it is needed by me*
den ska skrivas av dig *it will be written by you*
den lästes av honom *it was read by him*
den har trotts av alla *it has been believed by all*

ÖVNINGAR

I. Fyll i ord som fattas med nutid och översätt till engelska (Fill in the missing word with the present tense and translate into English).

1. Han _____ hem idag. (komma)
2. Hon _____ inte med henne. (tala)
3. Jag _____ för mycket. (arbeta)
4. De _____ resecheckar. (behöva)
5. Ni _____. (läsa)
6. Jag _____ dig. (tro)

II. Skriv de följande på svenska (Write the following in Swedish).

1. I have booked a room.
2. Are you Mr. Andersson?
3. Nice to meet you.
4. Pardon me, where is the hotel?
5. Would you like a cup of coffee?

III. Fyll i orden som fattas med dåtid för de svaga verben och översätt till engelska (Fill in the missing words with the past tense for these weak verbs and translate into English).

1. Jag _____ igår. (arbeta)
2. Du _____ mitt nummer. (behöva)
3. Han _____ ett rum. (boka)
4. Vad _____ han? (heta)
5. Var _____ du henne? (träffa)
6. _____ du med honom? (tala)

IV. Skriv de följande på svenska (Write the following in Swedish).

1. I will not be going.
2. I must write to her.
3. You will need that tomorrow.

4. He would read, but he cannot.
5. It was needed by me.

V. Fyll i orden som fattas med dåtid för de starka verben och översätt till engelska (Fill in the missing words with the past tense for these strong verbs and translate into English).

1. _____ du bra? (sova)
2. Han _____ inte. (komma)
3. Hon _____ på svenska. (skriva)
4. Ni _____. (binda)
5. Jag _____ inte den. (finna)

VI. Fyll i orden som fattas med perfekt för de verben och översätt till engelska (Fill in the missing word with the perfect for these verbs and translate into English).

1. Jag _____ med honom. (tala)
2. Du _____ hem. (komma)
3. _____ du _____ till henne? (skriva)
4. De _____ mig. (tro)
5. Hon _____ boken. (läsa)
6. Han _____ dig. (ringa)

VII. Byt följande meningar till s-passiv och översätt till engelska (Change the following sentences to the passive tense and translate into English).

1. Jag behöver boken.
2. Du skrev den.
3. Alla har trott det.
4. Hon läser det.

ETYMOLOGY

The verbal system in Swedish is similar to, but in fact easier than English. Like English, Swedish uses modal verbs to form its tenses: *har kommit* is in English *has come* and *ska komma* is English *will come*. The reason it can be seen as easier than English is because Swedish does not have all the periphrastic constructions. Whereas English regularly uses constructions like *is going*, Swedish does not. In Swedish one can only say *går*, literally *goes*. Further, Swedish does not have a form like *does go*. Thus, English forms its questions in the following way: *Are you going?* or *Did you go?*, but in Swedish one simply says: *Går du?* and *Gick du?* Therefore all the following sentences in English, *I go*, *I do go*, and *I am going*, translate into Swedish as simply *Jag går*.

English for most verbs has two forms for the present tense: *I, we, you, they go*; but *he, she, it goes*. Swedish only has one pattern for the present tense formed with *-r*. Interestingly, the present tense *-r* is in fact related to the English *-s*. Even the convoluted English verb *to be* with its *I am, you are, he/she/it is* construction is in Swedish only *är*, which is related to the English word *are*.

The word *ska*, also spelled *skall*, is related to the English word *shall*. The observant speaker of English will notice that words in Swedish with *sk* are often *sh* in English. That is because English at a rather early time underwent a sound change and all *sk* sounds became *sh*. Modern English words with *sk* are all loan words, borrowed after this early shift. Sometimes when English borrowed words from Old Scandinavian the words borrowed were cognates, or had the same meaning. Through time these words that originally had the same meaning shifted to two different meanings. This is why we have the word *shirt* from Old English meaning the top of a garment and skirt from Old Scandinavian meaning the bottom of the garment.

A Short History

Sweden has a long and rich history. The Viking age is said to have started around 800. The Danes and Norwegians went west to England, Ireland, the Faroes, Iceland, Greenland, and briefly making their way to the new world at L'Anse aux meadows at Newfoundland nearly 500 years before Christopher Columbus. The Swedes went east. The Swedish Vikings traveled through the interior of what is today Russia, down the Dnieper and the Volga making their way to Constantinople. Even the name of modern Russia is taken from the ancient name for the Swedes in this area, Rus meaning Red for the color of their hair. They etched out kingdoms and founded cities like Kiev and Novgorod, the last part of which, *gorod*, is the Russian pronunciation of the Old Swedish word *gård* meaning place or yard.

The Viking period ended during the twelfth century. During this period Christianity came to Sweden. Saint Erik, the patron saint of Sweden, was martyred in an attempt to convert the country. Several Swedish kings were killed by the nobles and the populace during the conversion period. They did not want to give up the old gods, but eventually they did and were fully Christianized by the thirteenth century, though many folk beliefs remained from the pre-Christian period.

The fifteenth century was a time of union. The Danish Queen, Margaret I, became the ruler for all three Scandinavian countries, Norway, Denmark, and Sweden in 1387. In 1389 she declared her sister's grandson, Erik, the king of Norway while she remained regent. By 1396 he had become heir apparent of Denmark and Sweden as well, and in 1397, on Trinity Sunday, June 17, in the Swedish city of Kalmar Erik was crowned the king of all three countries. This union was called the Kalmar union, and it was to last until 1523.

Though Norway and Denmark remained under the same monarch until the nineteenth century, the Kalmar union was a turbulent one with regards to Sweden and Denmark. In the early sixteenth century a young nobleman,

Gustav Eriksson, fought against the Danes in Sten Sture's army. He was captured and sent to a prison in Lübeck in what is today Germany. During his captivity he made friends with German merchants and learned of a priest named Martin Luther, an event that would prove important later in his life. In 1519 Gustav fled his captivity and returned to Sweden. After Sten Sture's death, Christian II of Denmark ruled all Sweden except Stockholm. Gustav Eriksson pleaded with the men of Dalarna to aid in his cause, but to no avail. Gustav fled to Norway on skis, but during this flight the men of Dalarna learned that Christian II had killed his opponents in Stockholm in what today is called the "Stockholm bloodbath." They skied after Gustav from Mora to the Norwegian border in what is to this day commemorated in a ski race called "Vasaloppet." Gustav was joined by mercenaries sent by the merchants he had befriended in Lübeck who feared Denmark's growing power. After he succeeded in defeating Christian II, Gustav gave himself the name Vasa and declared himself king. However, he still had several problems. Gustav Vasa needed to be approved by the Pope in Rome, there was doubt that this would happen, and he resented Rome's influence. He needed to pay the mercenaries. He also noticed that the church lands were about 36% of the national holdings, whereas his own were only about 5%. Remembering his encounter with the ideas of Martin Luther, he declared himself the head of the church, confiscated much of the church lands, paid his mercenaries and became the first monarch of a Protestant country.

The sixteenth and seventeenth centuries saw the rise of Sweden as an imperial power rivaled only by France. War was due to both the expansion of the Empire, started by Gustav Vasa, coupled with a Catholic/Lutheran conflict. This was a period of great territorial gain, cultural plunder, and two centuries of warfare. The age of Empire in the seventeenth century was heralded in by Gustav II Adolf, who succeeded his father as king in 1611 at the age of 16. He began a series of campaigns that brought Sweden into the fore as a major European empire. He resolved internal and external problems to Sweden's advantage by defeating Denmark and the Northern German states, as well as dissenting nobility within Sweden. Gustav II Adolf began expanding the empire by embroiling Sweden in war with the German states, Russia, and the Baltic states. Sweden's influence went East into what is today modern Russia and Prague, and South to Munich. In 1630, Gustav II Adolf became involved in the Thirty Years' War and was called "The Lion of the North." This hero of the Lutheran cause set his daughter to become Queen after his death.

Ironically, she converted to Catholicism and was, therefore, forced to abdicate, thus ending the Vasa Royal line.

The wars of the seventeenth century took a tremendous toll on the resources of Sweden. Nonetheless, Sweden made great strides in science and culture during the eighteenth century. Anders Celsius brought us the temperature scale that bears his name and the botanist Carl Linné created the latin classification system that is the foundation of the one used today. Gustav III was interested in art and culture and wanted Sweden to rival France in the south. If Louis XIV was to be known as "The Sun King" then he would be known as "The North Star King." After all the sun went down every night, whereas the north star was always up. In 1786 he founded the Swedish Academy, which would one day administer the Nobel prizes. In 1791 Gustav III tried to pit the European monarchs against the French Revolution. He wished to reinstate the absolute monarchy of the past. A conspiracy to assassinate the king succeeded when he was shot at the Stockholm opera house on March 16, 1792. The death of Gustav III two weeks later ended the Holstein-Gottorp line and Sweden's role as a major European power.

The poverty and loss of life that had concluded the Swedish imperial era shaped the national psyche in a way that lasts to this day. It is in part the explanation of Swedish neutrality during the First and Second World Wars. At the beginning of the nineteenth century Sweden fought its final war with Russia during the Napoleonic wars. As a result it lost its final colony, Finland. Because Sweden sided against Napoleon, however, and since Denmark had fought with France, Sweden was awarded Norway as compensation. Norway and Sweden were united under a single king until 1905. The nineteenth century was also a high time for Swedish literature and art. In 1896, Alfred Nobel, the inventor of dynamite, left the bulk of his wealth to a trust and began the Nobel prizes to be given in Physics, Medicine, Chemistry, Literature, and Peace. A prize in economics was added in 1968 by a donation from the Swedish riksbank.

The twentieth century has seen the rise of the Swedish welfare state, which will be discussed in subsequent chapters. Today Sweden is a modern country that enjoys a standard of living amongst the highest in the world.

LESSON

3

SAMTAL I

På restaurangen.

Fru Lindquist träffar Herr Andersson vid receptionen. Tillsammans går de till restaurangen.

HERR ANDERSSON: God kväll. Vi har beställt bord på namnet Andersson.

SERVITÖREN: Ja visst. Går det bra med det här bordet?

HERR ANDERSSON: Visst. Skulle fru Lindquist vilja ha en drink först?

FRU LINDQUIST: Ja tack. Jag tror jag skulle vilja ha ett glas vitt vin, kanske Chardonnay.

HERR ANDERSSON: Bra. Damen vill ha ett glas Chardonnay och jag vill ha en lättöl, Pripps blå. Tack.

De läser båda igenom menyn:

HERR ANDERSSON: Vad tror du du skulle vilja ha? Kött eller fisk?

FRU LINDQUIST: Nå, allt ser gott ut. Jag tror att jag skulle vilja ha fisk. Kanske torsk.

SERVITÖREN: Har ni bestämt er?

HERR ANDERSSON: Damen vill ha torsk och jag vill ha biffstek tack.

SERVITÖREN: Mycket bra.

När de har ätit färdigt sina varmrätter återkommer servitören:

SERVITÖREN: Skulle ni vilja ha efterrätt eller kaffe?

DIALOGUE I

At the restaurant.

Ms. Lindquist meets Mr. Andersson at the reception in the hotel. Together they walk to the restaurant.

MR. ANDERSSON: Good evening. We have a reservation in the name of Andersson.

WAITER: Of course. Will this table be ok?

MR. ANDERSSON: Yes, of course. Would you like a drink first Ms. Lindquist?

MS. LINDQUIST: Yes, thank you. I think I would like to have a glass of white wine, perhaps a Chardonnay.

MR. ANDERSSON: Fine. Then the lady will have a glass of Chardonnay and I will have a light beer. Pripps blue. Thanks.

They both read through the menu:

MR. ANDERSSON: What do you think you would like to have? Meat or fish?

MS. LINDQUIST: Well it all looks good. I think I would like to have fish. Perhaps the cod.

WAITER: Have you decided then?

MR. ANDERSSON: The lady will have the cod and I will have the steak please.

WAITER: Very good.

After they have finished their main courses the waiter returns.

WAITER: Would you like to have dessert or coffee?

HERR ANDERSSON: Jag skulle vilja ha en kopp kaffe, tack.

FRU LINDQUIST: Jag vill inte ha någonting, tack.

Herr Andersson ber om notan:

HERR ANDERSSON: Ursäkta mig, men skulle jag kunna få notan tack.

SERVITÖREN: Ja visst. Varsågod.

MR. ANDERSSON: I would like a cup of coffee, please.

MS. LINDQUIST: Nothing for me please.

Mr. Andersson asks for the bill:

MR. ANDERSSON: Excuse me, but could I have the bill, please?

WAITER: Of course. Here it is.

SAMTAL II

Eva träffar Vince på kaféet. De är båda lite hungriga och de bestämmer sig för att äta lite innan de går hem:

SERVITÖREN: Hej. Vad kan jag stå till tjänst med?

EVA: Ja, vi vill ha någonting att äta. Jag tar en räksmörgås och min kompis tar en pizza.

SERVITÖREN: Fint. Något att dricka? En öl eller Ramlösa?

EVA: Jag tar en Ramlösa. (*Till Vince*) Det är mineralvatten. Vince vad vill du ha?

VINCE: Jag tar en Coca-Cola.

EVA: Visst tar amerikanen Coca-Cola.

Några få minuter senare:

SERVITÖREN: Varsågoda. En räksmörgås och en pizza, en Ramlösa och en Coca-Cola. Något mer?

EVA: Nej tack. Hur mycket blir det?

SERVITÖREN: Det blir etthundrafemtio kronor.

EVA: Här är tvåhundra kronor.

SERVITÖREN: Och femtio tillbaka.

EVA: Tack.

SERVITÖREN: Tack.

DIALOGUE II

Eva meets Vince at the café. They are both a little hungry and decide to stay and get something small to eat before going home:

WAITER: Hello. What can I help you with?

EVA: Yes, we would like something to eat. I will take a shrimp sandwich and a pizza for my friend.

WAITER: Great. Something to drink? A beer or a glass of Ramlösa?

EVA: I will have a Ramlösa. (*To Vince*) That's mineral water. Vince, what do you want?

VINCE: I would like a Coca-Cola.

EVA: Of course the American would have a Coca-Cola.

A few minutes later:

WAITER: Here you are. A shrimp sandwich and a pizza, one Ramlösa and a Coca-Cola. Anything else?

EVA: No thank you. How much is that?

WAITER: That will be 150 crowns.

EVA: Here is 200.

WAITER: And 50 back.

EVA: Thanks.

WAITER: Thanks.

VOCABULARY

allt *pro.*	ahllt	everything
amerikan *n. com.*	ahmehrik**ahn**	American
att *conj.*	ahtt	that
be IV (bad-bett) *v.*	beh	ask
beställa *v.*	behst**eh**llah	reserve
bestämma *v.* (*ref.*)	behst**eh**mmah	decide
biffstek 2 *n. com.*	biffstayk	beef steak
bli V (blir-blev-blivit) *v.*	blee	become
blå *adj.*	blao	blue
bord 5 *n. neu.*	bohrd	table
båda *adj.*	b**oa**dah	both
dam 2 *n. com.*	daam	lady
dricka IV i-a-u *v.*	drickah	drink
drink 2 *n. com.*	drink	alcoholic drink
då *adv.*	doa	then
efter *prep.*	**eh**ftehr	after
efterrätt 3 *n. com.*	**eh**ftehrr**eh**tt	dessert
eller *conj.*	**eh**llehr	or
etthundrafemtio	**eh**tthundraaf**eh**mti	one hundred and fifty
femtio	f**eh**mti	fifty
fint *adj. neu.*	fint	fine/great
fisk 2 *n. com.*	fisk	fish
få *adj.*	foa	few
få IV (får-fick-fått) *v.*	foa	get
färdigt *adj. neu.*	f**eh**rdeet	finished
först *adj.*	f**err**sht	first
glas 5 *n. neu.*	glaas	glass
god *adj.*	goo	good
gott *adj. neu.*	gohtt	good
hem 5 *n. neu.*	hehm	home
hungrig *adj.*	hungrig	hungry
hur *inter.*	hewr	how
i *prep.*	ee	in
ingenting 5 *n. neu.*	ingehnting	nothing

innan *prep.*	innahn	before
kafé 5 (-er) *n. neu.*	kahfeh	café
kaffe 5 *n. neu.*	kahffeh	coffee
kanske *adv.*	kahnsheh	maybe
kopp 2 *n. com.*	kop	cup
kväll 2 *n com.*	kvehll	evening
kött 5 *n. neu.*	shertt	meat
lite *adv.*	leeteh	a little
läsa IIb *v.*	lehsah	read
lättöl 5 *n. neu.*	lehtterl	light beer
meny (*pl.* menyer) *n. neu.*	mehniw	menu
mer *adj.*	mehr	more
nota 1 *n. com.*	nootah	check/bill
nå *intj.*	noa	well
någonting 5 *n. neu.*	noanting	something
något *adj. neu.*	noat	something
några *adj. pl.*	noarah	anything
pizza 1 *n. com.*	pitssah	pizza
Pripps blå	pripps bloa	a Swedish beer
på *prep.*	poa	on
Ramlösa	raamlersah	a Swedish mineral water
räkning 2 *n. com.*	rehkkning	check/bill
räksmörgås *n. com.*	rehksmerrgoas	shrimp sandwich
se ut *v.*	say ewt	look (like)
senare *adj.*	saynahreh	later
servitör 3 *n. com.*	sehrviterr	waiter
sina *pro. pl.*	seenah	his/her own
stanna I *v.*	stahnnah	stay
stå III *v.*	stoa	stand
ta V (tar-tog-tagit) *v.*	taa	take
till *prep.*	till	to
tillbaka *adv.*	tillbaakah	back
tillsammans *adv.*	tillsahmmahns	together
tjänst 3 *n. com.*	shehnst	service
torsk 2 *n. com.*	tohrshk	cod
tro III *v.*	troo	believe
träffa I *v.*	trehffah	meet

tvåhundra	tvoahundrah	two hundred
tycka IIb *v.*	tikkah	believe
ursäkta I *v.*	ewrshehktah	excuse
ut *adv.*	ewt	out (direction)
vad *inter.*	vah	what
varmrätt 3 *n. com.*	vahrmreht	main course
varsågod	vahrsoagoo	here you are
vid *prep.*	veed	at/by
vilja V (vill-ville-velat) *v.*	vilyah	want
vin (*pl.* viner) *n. neu.*	veen	wine
visst *adv.*	visst	of course
åt *prep.*	oat	for/at
återkomma IV o-o-o *v.*	oatehrkohmmah	return
äta IV ä-å-ä *v.*	aehtah	eat
öl 5 *n. neu.*	erl	beer

USEFUL EXPRESSIONS

Jag skulle vilja beställa bord.	I would like to reserve a table.
Kan jag få se menyn?	May I see the menu?
Vad föreslår du?	What do you recommend?
Jag skulle vilja ha ...	I would like to have ...
biff	beef
oxfilé	beef fillet
kalvfilé	veal fillet
fläskkarré	pork loin
griskotlett	pork chop
skinka	ham
lamm	lamb
korv	sausages/hot dogs
kyckling	chicken
lax	salmon
flundra	flounder
torsk	cod
sill	herring
rödspätta	plaice
räkor	shrimp
hummer	lobster
krabba	crab
bröd	bread
frukt	fruit
ost	cheese
efterrätt	dessert
kaffe	coffee
Jag har ...	I don't have a ...
ingen kniv	knife
ingen gaffel	fork
ingen sked	spoon
ingen servett	napkin
Skulle jag kunna få notan tack?*	Could I have the check please?
Var ligger toaletterna?	Where are the bathrooms?

*The word *räkningen* is also used in some areas.

GRAMMAR

1. Adjectives

Adjectives, like nouns, decline or have different forms depending on whether they are neuter (*ett*), common (*en*), plural, definite or indefinite. The good news is that the definite and plural forms are the same, so the student only needs worry about the indefinite singular forms.

en **stor** flicka *a big girl*   två **stora** flickor *two big girls*
den **stora** flickan *the big girl*   de **stora** flickorna *the big girls*

ett **stort** barn *a big child*   två **stora** barn *two big children*
det **stora** barnet *the big child*   de **stora** barnen *the big children*

Again, notice that the only tricky forms are indefinite singular: *en stor flicka* and *ett stort barn*. When used with the verb *to be* the adjective is considered to be indefinite:

en flicka är **stor** *a girl is big*
två flickor är **stora** *two girls are big*
ett barn är **stort** *a child is big*
två barn är **stora** *two children are big*

There are a few adjectives that need comment since they do unusual but predictable things:

1.   Adjectives ending in -*d* that are preceded by a consonant drop the -*d* before the *t*-ending in the neuter:

en hård dag *a hard day*
ett hårt äpple *a hard apple*
dagen var hård *the day was hard*
äpplet var hårt *the apple was hard*

2.   Adjectives ending in *-d* that are preceded by a vowel drop the *-d* and
        add *-tt*:

    en röd bil *a red car*
    ett rött hus *a red house*
    bilen var röd *the car was red*
    huset var rött *the house was red*

Rules 1 and 2 are not so strange since the sounds *d* and *t* are made at the
same place in the mouth and therefore the spelling merely reflects the fact
that you cannot say *d* and *t* together.

3.   Adjectives ending in unstressed *-en* drop the *-n* before taking the *-t*:

    en mogen pojke *a mature boy*
    ett moget barn *a mature child*
    pojken var mogen *the boy was mature*
    barnet var moget *the child was mature*

4.   Adjectives ending in a stressed vowel take *–tt*, thereby shortening the
        vowel:

    en ny bil *a new car*
    ett nytt hus *a new house*
    bilen var ny *the car was new*
    huset var nytt *the house was new*

5.   Adjectives ending in *-t* preceded by another consonant do not double the *t*:

    en brant backe *a steep hill*
    ett brant stup *a steep precipice*
    backen var brant *the hill was steep*
    stupet var brant *the precipice was steep*
  but
    en vit flagga *a white flag*
    ett vitt hus *a white house*

6. Adjectives already ending in *-tt* do not add another *t*:

en trött pojke *a tired boy*
ett trött barn *a tired child*
pojken var trött *the boy was tired*
barnet var trött *the child was tired*

7. Finally, there are a few adjectives that do not decline:

en bra flicka *a good girl*
två bra flickor *two good girls*
ett bra barn *a good child*
två bra barn *two good children*

2. Possessive Pronouns

Possessive pronouns are adjectives. First and second person possessive pronouns are, therefore, declined for gender and number:

min bil *my car*   mina bilar *my cars*
mitt hus *my house*   mina hus *my houses*

din bil *your car*   dina bilar *your cars*
ditt hus *your house*   dina hus *your houses*

vår bil *our car*   våra bilar *our cars*
vårt hus *our house*   våra hus *our houses*

er bil *your car*   era bilar *your cars*
ert hus *your house*   era hus *your houses*

but third person possessive pronouns do not decline for gender and number:

hans bil *his car*   hans bilar *his cars*
hans hus *his house*   hans hus *his houses*

hennes bil *her car*   hennes bilar *her cars*
hennes hus *her house*   hennes hus *her houses*

deras bil *their car*   deras bilar *their cars*
deras hus *their house*   deras hus *their houses*

When including other adjectives with these phrases the adjectives are definite since, after all, you know whose it is. However, if the adjective follows the verb, it is indefinite:

min vita bil *my white car*
mina vita bilar *my white cars*
mitt vita hus *my white house*
mina vita hus *my white houses*
but
min bil är vit *my car is white*
mina bilar är vita *my cars are white*
mitt hus är vitt *my house is white*
mina hus är vita *my houses are white*

3.   Possessive Nouns

To form the possessive simply add an -*s* , without an apostrophe, to the end of the word as you would in English:

Evas bil *Eva's car*
flickornas hus *the girls' house*
pojkens bil *the boy's car*

As with possessive pronouns, when including adjectives with these phrases the adjectives are definite. However, if the adjective follows the verb, it is indefinite:

Evas röda bil *Eva's red car*
flickornas fina hus *the girls' fine house*
pojkens vita bil *the boy's white car*
but:
Evas bil är röd *Eva's car is red*
flickornas hus är fint *the girls' house is fine*
pojkens bil är vit *the boy's car is white*

ÖVNINGAR

I. Fyll i orden som fattas med de rätta possessiva adjektiven (Fill in the missing words with the correct possessive adjectives).

1. (my) _____ bil.
2. (your) _____ hus.
3. (his) _____ äpple.
4. (their) _____ pojke.
5. (her) _____ kopp.
6. (our) _____ bok.

II. Skriv de rätta formen av de obestämda adjektiven (Write the correct form of the indefinite adjective).

1. Huset är _____ (big).
2. Barnet är _____ (tired).
3. Bilen är _____ (new).
4. Hotellet är _____ (expensive).
5. Vinet är _____ (good).

III. Översätt till svenska (Translate into Swedish).

1. I would like to have a glass of wine.
2. We have reserved a table.
3. I would like to have the fish
4. I would like a cup of coffee.
5. Excuse me, but could I have the check?
6. How much is that?

IV. Fyll i rätt form av de bestämda adjektiven (Write the correct form of the definite adjective).

1. Det _____ huset är där (big).
2. Det _____ barnet ska sova nu (tired).
3. Den _____ bilen är röd (new).

4. Har du stannat på det _____ hotellet (expensive).
5. Vi drack det _____ vinet (good).

V. Översätt till engelska (Translate into English).

1. Vad heter du?
2. Har ni bestämt er?
3. Något att dricka?
4. Skulle ni ha något mer?
5. Ville ni ha räkningen?

ETYMOLOGY

English no longer declines its adjectives the way Swedish does. There are no forms like *stor* for one type of noun and *stort* for another. Likewise we no longer have different genders for nouns. Students have asked how *en* and *ett* relate to the masculine and feminine that they have encountered in other languages. Whereas *ett* is what some linguists have called neuter, *en* is called common. This is because Swedish several hundred years ago conflated masculine and feminine into one gender, *en*. Of course English has conflated masculine, feminine, and neuter into one gender making the concept of gender meaningless.

English owes much to loans from the Scandinavian languages, including, strangely enough, our third person plural pronoun. The Old English third person plural pronoun was *hie*. As time went one and sound changes occured, *hie* became too easily confused with *he*. The solution, due to the fact that there were many Scandinavians living in England at the time, was to borrow the Old Scandinavian word, *their*, and thus our word became *they*.

Politics and Government

The Swedish parliament, Riksdag, has consisted of a single chamber since 1971. It has 349 members elected to four-year terms. A member of the Riksdag is elected by the party and placed on that party's list of candidates in one of Sweden's 29 constituencies. The public cast their votes for a party, although they can also cast a vote for individual candidates by putting a cross next to their name on the party list. Sweden has a proportional parliament. This means that all parties are allocated seats in proportion to the number of votes they received in the general election. There is a minimum of 4% to gain members to parliament thereby limiting the number of small parties in Riksdag. Until recently there were five parties in parliament: *Vänsterpartiet*—the left party; *Socialdemokraterna*—the Social Democrats; *Centerpartiet*—the Center Party; *Folkpartiet*—the Liberal Party; and *Moderaterna*—the Moderates. Recently there have been two new parties on the Swedish political scene, namely the Christian Democratic Party and the Green Party. Since no party holds a majority, government is formed by coalitions between parties with similar political agendas. Sweden has the highest proportion of women members in parliament. In 2001 it was 43%.

Sweden is a constitutional monarchy. Therefore the annual session of the parliament is opened by the king each September or, in an election year, in early October. Riksdag holds its sessions all year with two breaks, one over Christmas and one in the summer. The prime minister position is held by the party with the greatest number of votes. The prime minister delivers a policy speech outlining the government's programs for the coming year at the opening of the parliament. The speaker is the second highest office held, after the king, who holds no political power but is the head of state. The speaker is elected by the parliament. The speaker is the Riksdag's main representative, directing business and presiding over meetings of the chamber. The speaker also develops the work procedures and represents the Riksdag both in Sweden and abroad. Importantly, the speaker, like the king, is impartial in relation to the different parties and for this reason he or she is not permitted to take part in debates or vote on matters before the parliament. The speaker leads negotiations in the event the government resigns. After consulting representatives of all political parties and the deputy speaker, the speaker presents a proposal for a new prime minister to the parliament for approval.

In 1995 Sweden voted to become a member of the European Union in a general election. Since this decision, Sweden has played an influential role in European Union politics. However, Sweden has elected not to take part in the European currency and keeps its monetary unit, which is called the *krona*.

LESSON
4

SAMTAL I

På stan.

Det är lördag och Herr Andersson ska visa fru Lindquist Stockholm. Fru Lindquist läser ur en turistbok hon köpte i en affär:

FRU LINDQUIST: Otroligt. Det står här att det finns 24 000 öar i Stockholms skärgård.

HERR ANDERSSON: Det är riktigt, och i juni 2002 firade Stockholm 750 års jubileum. Stockholm har kallats för Nordens Venedig. Vad ville du se?

FRU LINDQUIST: Jag tror att jag skulle vilja se alla viktiga ställen och sedan vill jag gå runt i Gamla Stan.

HERR ANDERSSON: Okej då. Låt oss börja med Stadshuset där de delar ut Nobelprisen.

FRU LINDQUIST: Vet du var det är?

HERR ANDERSSON: Jag vet inte hur man går dit, men vi kan fråga någon. (*Till mannen på gatan*) Ursäkta mig. Hur kommer man till Stadshuset?

MANNEN PÅ GATAN: Det är lite långt. Du kan gå dit men det är ungefär en kilometer. Gå ner för Kungsgatan ända till Kungsbron och sväng sedan till höger. Gå sedan ner för Kungsbrostrand till Serafimerstrand och där är det.

HERR ANDERSSON: Tack. Nu kommer jag ihåg.

DIALOGUE I

On the town.

It is Saturday and Mr. Andersson is going to show Ms. Lindquist Stockholm. Ms. Lindquist reads from a guide book she bought in a shop:

MS. LINDQUIST: Unbelievable. It says here that in Stockholm's archipelago there are 24,000 islands.

MR. ANDERSSON: That's right, and in June 2002 Stockholm celebrated its 750th anniversary. Stockholm has been called the Venice of the north. What would you like to see?

MS. LINDQUIST: I think I would like to see all the important places and then to walk around the old town.

MR. ANDERSSON: Ok, then let's start with the City Hall, which is where they give the Nobel Prizes.

MS. LINDQUIST: Do you know where it is?

MR. ANDERSSON: I don't know how to walk there, but we can ask someone. (*To a man on the street*) Excuse me, how does one walk to the City Hall?

MAN ON THE STREET: Hmm, it's a little far. You can walk there, but it is about a kilometer. Walk down King's Street all the way until King's Bridge and then turn left. Walk down King's Bridge Shore all the way until The Shore of the Order of the Seraph and it is right there.

MR. ANDERSSON: Thanks. Now I remember.

Herr Andersson och fru Lindquist tittar på Stadshuset och efteråt säger fru Lindquist:

FRU LINDQUIST: Det var en lång promenad. Nu vill jag gärna sitta ner en stund och vila.

HERR ANDERSSON: Det finns en stadsbåttur. Där kan vi sitta. Ville du ta den?

FRU LINDQUIST: Det var en bra idé.

Mr. Andersson and Ms. Lindquist see the City Hall and afterwards Ms. Lindquist says:

Ms. LINDQUIST: That was a long walk. Now I would really like to sit down for a while and rest.

MR. ANDERSSON: There are some boat tours of the city. We could sit there. Would you like to take one?

Ms. LINDQUIST: That is a good idea.

SAMTAL II

Vince vill gärna se Göteborg. Han går till tågstationen till turistinformationen där:

VINCE: Har du en karta över stan?

INFORMATIONEN: Ja. Här får du en.

VINCE: Tack. Jag skulle gärna se stan till fots. Jag är lite rädd för att det ska börja regna.

INFORMATIONEN: Kyrkorna är öppna. Du kan gå in i någon av dem.

VINCE: Är museerna öppna idag?

INFORMATIONEN: Ja, de har öppet från klockan nio till klockan sjutton.

VINCE: Finns det någonting speciellt som pågår idag?

INFORMATIONEN: Det finns nästa vecka. Men ingenting nu, nej.

VINCE: Synd. Finns det en rundtur av stan?

INFORMATIONEN: Ja visst. Om du vill kan jag ge dig all nödvändig information. Jag kan högt rekommendera Göteborgskortet, med det får du rabatter på många museer. Du borde också gå på nöjesparken Liseberg.

VINCE: Tack.

DIALOGUE II

Vince really wants to see Gothenburg. He goes to the train station to the tourist information kiosk there:

VINCE: Do you have a map of the city?

INFORMATION: Yes. Here, you can have one.

VINCE: Thank you. I would like to see the city on foot. I am a little afraid it may rain though.

INFORMATION: The churches are open. You can always go into one of them.

VINCE: Are the museums open today?

INFORMATION: Yes, they are open from 9:00 to 17:00.

VINCE: Is there anything special going on today?

INFORMATION: There is next week. But nothing now, no.

VINCE: That's too bad. Are there any tours of the city?

INFORMATION: Yes, of course. If you like, I can give you the necessary information. I can highly recommend the Gothenburg card, with it you will get rebates at many of the museums. Also, you should be sure to go to the amusement park, Liseberg.

VINCE: Thanks.

VOCABULARY

affär 3 *n. com.*	ahff**ehr**	store/business
alla *pro.*	**ah**llah	everyone
av *prep.*	aav	by/of
böra V (bör-borde-bort) *v.*	b**err**ah	ought
börja I *v.*	b**err**jah	begin
dela ut I *v.*	d**eh**lah ewt	to give out
då *adv.*	doa	then
efteråt *adv.*	ehftehr**oat**	afterwards
fira I *v.*	f**eer**ah	to celebrate
från *prep.*	fr**aon**	from
Gamla Stan	gahmlaa st**ahn**	old town
gata 1 *n. com.*	g**aa**tah	street
gärna *adv.*	y**eh**rnah	willingly
hålla IV å-ö-å *v.*	h**oh**llah	hold
höger *adv.*	h**er**gehr	right
högt *adv.*	h**er**kt	highly
idag *adv.*	eed**ah**	today
idé 3 *n. com.*	eed**ay**	idea
in *adv.*	in	inside
information 3 *n. com.*	infohrmaash**oon**	information
jo *intj.*	joo	yes
jubileum (*pl.* jubiléer)	jubil**eh**um	anniversary
n. neu.		
juni	j**ew**nee	June
kallas I *v.*	k**ah**llahs	be called
karta 1 *n. com.*	k**ah**rtah	map
komma ihåg *v.*	k**oh**mmah eeh**oag**	remember
Kungsbro	kungsbr**oo**	King's Bridge
Kungsgatan	kungsg**aa**tahn	King's Street
kyrka 1 *n. com.*	k**iw**rkah	church
köpa IIb *v.*	sh**er**pah	buy
lång *adj.*	l**oh**ngg	long
långt *adv.*	l**oh**ngkt	long
låta IV å-ä-å *v.*	l**oa**tah	allow/let

lördag	lerrdah	Saturday
museum 3 (*pl.* muséer) *n. neu.*	mewsehum	museum
många *adj.*	moangah	many
ner *adv.*	nehr	down
nio	neeah	nine
Nobelpris 3 *n. com.*	nohbehlprees	Nobel prize
Norden	nohrdehn	Nordic Countries
nu *adv.*	new	now
någon *pro.*	noan	someone
någon *adj.*	noan	some
nästa *adj.*	nehstah	next
nödvändig *adj.*	nerdvehndig	necessary
nöjespark 2 *n. com.*	neryehspahrk	amusement park
också *adv.*	ohksoh	also
otroligt *adv.*	ohtroolit	unbelievable
promenad 3 *n. com.*	prohmehnaad	walk
pågå V (~går- ~gick-~gått) *v.*	poagoa	going on
rabatt 3 *n. com.*	rahbahtt	rebate
regna I *v.*	rehgnah	rain
rekommendera I *v.*	rehkohmehndehrah	recommend
riktigt *adv.*	riktit	right
rundtur 3 *n. com.*	rundtewr	sightseeing tour
runt *adv.*	runt	around
rädd *adj.*	rehdd	afraid
se V (såg-sett) *v.*	say	see
sedan *adv.*	sehn	later
Serafimerstrand	sehraafeemehrstrahnd	The Shore of the Order of the Seraph
sitta IV i-a-u *v.*	sittah	sit
sjutton	shuttohn	seventeen
skärgård 2 *n. com.*	shehrgohrd	archipelago
speciellt *adj. neu.*	spehseeehllt	special
stadsbåttur 3 *n. com.*	stahtsboattewr	city boat tour
Stadshuset	stahtshewseht	the City Hall
stad (*pl.* städer) *n. com.*	staad	city
stan	staan	the city

strand 3 *n. com.*	strahnd	shore/beach
stund 3 *n. com.*	stund	moment
ställe 4 *n. neu.*	stehlleh	place
svänga IIa *v.*	svehngah	turn
synd *adj.*	siwnd	too bad/pity
säga V (säger-sa-sagt) *v.*	sehya	say
tills *conj.*	tills	until
titta på *v.*	tittah poa	look at
turistbok (*pl.* -böcker) *n. com.*	tewreestbook	guide book
turistinformation 3 *n. com.*	tewreestinfohrmahshoon	tourist information
tågstation 3 *n. com.*	toagstahshoon	train station
ungefär *adv.*	unyehfehr	about *or* approximately
vecka 1 *n. com.*	vehkkah	week
Venedig	vehnehdeeg	Venice
veta V (vet-visste-vetat) *v.*	vehtah	know
viktig *adj.*	viktig	important
visa I *v.*	veesah	show
år 5 *n. neu.*	ohr	year
ö 2 *n. com.*	er	island
öppen *adj.*	erppehn	open
över *prep.*	ervehr	over

USEFUL EXPRESSIONS

Kan du rekommendera någon tur?	Can you recommend a tour?
Var ligger...?	Where is/are the...?
nöjesparken	amusement park
konstgalleriet	art gallery
botaniska trädgården	botanical gardens
slottet	castle
domkyrkan	cathedral
kyrkan	church
konserthuset	concert hall
stadscentrum	downtown
utställningen	exhibition
biblioteket	library
muséet	museum
Gamla Stan	Old Town
operahuset	opera house
parken	park
riksdagshuset	parliament building
Kungliga Slottet	Royal palace
torget	square
teatern	theater
Hur dags öppnar det?	When does it open?
Hur dags stänger det?	When does it close?
Hur mycket kostar det?	How much does it cost?
Vad kostar inträdet?	How much is the entrance fee?
Var köper jag en biljett?	Where do I buy a ticket?

GRAMMAR

1. Numbers

The following are the numbers in Swedish:

	CARDINAL NUMBERS	ORDINAL NUMBERS
0	noll	
1	en/ett	första
2	två	andra
3	tre	tredje
4	fyra	fjärde
5	fem	femte
6	sex	sjätte
7	sju	sjunde
8	åtta	åttonde
9	nio	nionde
10	tio	tionde
11	elva	elfte
12	tolv	tolfte
13	tretton	trettonde
14	fjorton	fjortonde
15	femton	femtonde
16	sexton	sextonde
17	sjutton	sjuttonde
18	arton	artonde
19	nitton	nittonde
20	tjugo	tjugonde
21	tjugoen -ett	tjugoförsta
22	tjugotvå	tjugoandra
30	trettio	trettionde
40	fyrtio	fyrtionde
50	femtio	femtionde
60	sextio	sextionde

70	sjuttio	sjutionde
80	åttio	åttionde
90	nittio	nittionde
100	(ett) hundra	hundrade
101	hundraen -ett	hundraförsta
200	tvåhundra	tvåhundrade
1000	(ett) tusen	tusende
1001	(ett) tusenen -ett	tusenförsta
2000	tvåtusen	tvåtusende

1 000 000	en miljon
2 000 000	två miljoner
1 000 000 000	en miljard
2 000 000 000	två miljarder
1 000 000 000 000	en biljon
2 000 000 000 000	två biljoner

Note that *tjugoen* and *tjugotvå* etc. are pronounced *shewen* and *shewtvoa* etc. Also *trettio*, *fyrtio* etc. are pronounced *tretti* and *fyrti*, in other words the *o* at the end is seldom pronounced. Also, Swedish has spaces between large numbers rather than commas, thus ten thousand is written 10 000.

2. Time

In Swedish the speaker asks "what is the clock" or "how much is the clock." The clock is also seen as female, so when answering the speaker may say "she is two." Time is expressed much the same way as English with the exception of between 20 minutes after and to the hour. During that interval time is expressed in terms of the half hour:

Hur mycket är klockan? *How much is the clock/what time is it?*
Vad är klockan? *What is the clock/what time is it?*

Klockan är ett. *It is one o'clock.*
Det är två. *It is two o'clock.*
Hon är tre. *She is three o'clock.*

Klockan är fem över tre. *It is five past three.*
Klockan är kvart över fyra. *It is quarter past four.*
Klockan är tjugo över fem. *It is twenty past five.*
Klockan är fem i halv sex. *It is five to half six* or *It is twenty-five past five.*
Klockan är halv sex. *It is half past five.*
Klockan är fem över halv sex. *It is twenty-five to six.*
Klockan är kvart i sex. *It is quarter to six.*

Notice that at the half hour Swedish looks ahead to the coming hour rather than behind to the preceding, e.g. *halv sex* is five thirty.

3. Days of the Week

The days of the week are:

söndag	*Sunday*
måndag	*Monday*
tisdag	*Tuesday*
onsdag	*Wednesday*
torsdag	*Thursday*
fredag	*Friday*
lördag	*Saturday*

Note that in Swedish the days of the week are not capitalized.

4. Months of the Year

The months of the year are:

januari	*January*
februari	*February*
mars	*March*
april	*April*
maj	*May*
juni	*June*
juli	*July*
augusti	*August*
september	*September*

oktober   *October*
november *November*
december *December*

Again, the months are not capitalized in Swedish.

5. Dates

Here are a few comments on dates in Swedish. Swedish dates are often expressed in much the same way as English:

trettioförsta december nittonhundranittiotvå
31st of December 1992

It is also common in Swedish to describe the month by number:

femte i andra *fifth of February (February being the second month of the year)*
sjätte i sjunde *sixth of July (July being the seventh month of the year)*

Notice that there is no equivalent to *of* in Swedish.

Jag är född den sjuttonde juni nittonhundrasjuttiotvå.
I was born the 17th of June 1972.

Dates are written in Sweden day-month-year, not month-day-year as in American English, thus Dec. 2, 1972 is written 2 dec 1972; or sometime year-month-date. e.g. 1972-12-2.

Note that Swedish expresses centuries in the following manner:

på 1800-talet *in the nineteenth century*
på 1900-talet *in the twentieth century*
på 1990-talet *in the 1990s* or *in the '90s*

Andra världskriget var på 1900-talet.
The Second World War was in the twentieth century.

6. Money

Sweden has opted not to take the European Union currency called the Euro and will be keeping its own currency. The currency is called *krona* or sometimes in English called a *crown*. There is a smaller unit called *öre*. There are 100 *öre* in one *krona*, but since one *öre* has no value Sweden has rid itself of all its smaller denominations less than half a crown, or 50 *öre*. The coins that exist today are 50 *öre*, 1 *krona*, 5 *kronor*, and 10 *kronor*. The notes that exist today are 20 *kronor*, 100 *kronor*, 500 *kronor*, and 1000 *kronor* bills. Though exchange rates vary, the Swedish *kronor* usually ranges between 7 and 10 *kronor* to the dollar.

ÖVNINGAR

I.   Skriv ut följande siffror (Write out the following numbers).

    1. 8 _____.
    2. 17 _____.
    3. 534 _____.
    4. 726 _____.
    5. 1342 _____.
    6. 1 234 672 _____.

II. Skriv ut vilken tid det är (Write out what time it is).

    1. 10:00 _____.
    2. 11:20 _____.
    3. 12:25 _____.
    4. 1:35   _____.
    5. 4:40   _____.
    6. 5:45   _____.

III. Skriv ut följande datum (Write out the following dates).

    1. January 1   _____.
    2. February 3   _____.
    3. March 14   _____.
    4. June 22   _____.
    5. August 28   _____.
    6. December 31 _____.

IV. Översätt till svenska (Translate into Swedish).

    1. I would like to see all the important places.
    2. How do you get to the City Hall?
    3. Where can we sit and have a cup of coffee?
    4. Do you have a map of the city?
    5. Is there a city tour?

V. Översätt till engelska (Translate into English).

1. Det är en kilometer.
2. Gå rakt fram och sväng till vänster.
3. Det finns en stadsbåttur.
4. Det är lite långt att gå.
5. Museet är öppet klockan två.

ETYMOLOGY

The days of the week in both English and Swedish have their origins in pagan times. For the Germanic peoples, the concept of naming the days came from the Romans. They had named each day for a pagan god. The Germanic tribes adopted this idea, but named the days after their own gods. Sunday and Monday are named for the sun and the moon, Swedish *söndag* and *måndag*. Saturday is named for the Roman god Saturn in English. In Swedish *lördag* means washing day, since it was the day to wash clothes.

The other days of the week still bear the names of the old Germanic pagan gods in English and Swedish. Tuesday, *tisdag*, is named for the god of war, Tyr. A thousand year ago, he became more a god of justice and is the only god who was brave enough to put his hand in the ferocious wolf Fenrir's mouth when the wolf was to be bound. He lost his hand for that show of trust. Wednesday, Swedish *onsdag*, is named for the chief of the gods, Odin. He is known as the god with one eye, because he gave up his eye to drink from Mimir's well of wisdom. He is said to have given humanity writing and poetry. Thursday, Swedish *torsdag*, is named for the war god Thor. He is in constant vigilance to protect the gods and humans from the giants. Finally, Friday, Swedish *fredag*, is named for the love goddess Freyja.

Social Welfare

Swedish society is characterized by consensus and involvement. Swedish politics of the twentieth century can be called the politics of the social welfare state. At the end of the nineteenth century, the political debate in Sweden was dominated by the unions and the issue of the right to vote. In 1866 a parliamentary reform left only men who owned land with the right to vote in the country. This was largely seen as unacceptable by the unions and the general populace. The Social Democratic Party was founded in 1889 in order to address voting rights and it would have a tremendous influence in politics to the present day. Demands for universal suffrage were also made by the Liberal Party, formed in the 1890s, whose constituents were largely rural people. The Labor movement suffered a large setback due to the failure of general strikes in 1909. However, men were given the vote at that time. Universal suffrage was finally achieved in Sweden in 1919, at which time women were given the right to vote. Perhaps because the right was so hard-won, the percentage of eligible voters who voted in the last election was 81.4%.

The effects of the Great Depression were deeply felt in Sweden starting at the end of 1930. Working conditions, which had never been good, became worse than ever. The social welfare system that is in place today is in large part a result of that turbulent time and was their answer to the problems of that era in much the same way as Roosevelt's New Deal. The way the Swedes solved the problem of growing poverty was a redistribution of wealth through taxation and growth of employment in the public sector. Tax-financed consumption of goods and services rose from 12.5% to 30% from 1950 to 1980 while the number of public sector employees rose by one million. During the 1980s that level fell to 26.4%, though public sector employees increased by more than 100,000.

Today Sweden is characterized by an even distribution of income and wealth. In Sweden the difference in wealth from the poorest to the richest is a factor of one thousand, as opposed to a factor of one million in the United States. The public sector, which accounts for nearly a third of the labor force, accounts for a relatively large part of this redistribution. The public sector redistributes 27% of the Gross Domestic Product, whereas tax-finance consumption and capital spending absorb 29%. Naturally the result is a rather high tax base. However, Sweden has some of the highest rates of services in the world. National medical insurance, education through college, child care, and parental leave are but a few of the services offered to Swedes at little or no cost.

LESSON
5

SAMTAL I

Att hitta vägen.

Fru Lindquist lämnar Herr Andersson och går runt Stockholm på egen hand. Hon märker att hon har gått vilse och vill veta hur man kommer till Kungliga slottet:

FRU LINDQUIST: Ursäkta mig, får jag ställa en fråga?

KVINNAN PÅ GATAN: Ja visst.

FRU LINDQUIST: Jag försöker hitta till Kungliga slottet, skulle du kunna beskriva hur man kommer dit?

KVINNAN PÅ GATAN: Ja, det är inte långt. Det är nära kyrkan i Gamla Stan. Du är på Hamngatan ... gå ner längs gatan tills du kommer till Kungsträdgården och sväng sedan till höger. Du går genom gården och gatan byter namn till Strömbron. Gå över bron och slottet är på andra sidan.

Fru Lindquist hittar vägen dit och tittar på vaktombytet. Hon går genom Gamla Stans virrvarr av gatorna. När det är dags att gå tillbaka till hotellet, förstår hon att hon har gått vilse igen och måste fråga om vägen tillbaka till hotellet:

FRU LINDQUIST: Ursäkta mig, vet du var Hotell Kung Karl är?

GAMLA MANNEN: Ja, det är nära Stureplan på Birger Jarlsgatan.

FRU LINDQUIST: Hur kommer jag dit?

DIALOGUE I

Finding your way.

Ms. Lindquist leaves Mr. Andersson and goes walking around Stockholm on her own. She notices that she is lost and wants to know how to get to the Royal Castle:

MS. LINDQUIST: Excuse me, may I ask you a question?

WOMAN ON THE STREET: Of course.

MS. LINDQUIST: I am trying to find the Royal Castle, would you be able to tell me how to get there?

WOMAN ON THE STREET: Yes, it is not far. It is near the church, in the Old Town. You are on Harbor Street, go down along this street until you come to the Royal Garden Street and turn right. You will go through the garden and the street will change names and become Stream Bridge. Go over the bridge and the castle is on the other side.

Ms. Lindquist finds her way there and sees the changing of the guards. She walks through the maze-like streets of Old Town. When she is ready to go back to her hotel, she finds that she is lost again and must ask how to get back to her hotel:

MS. LINDQUIST: Excuse me, do you know where Hotel Kung Karl is?

OLD MAN: Yes, it is by Sture Square on Birger Jarl's Street.

MS. LINDQUIST: And how do I get there?

GAMLA MANNEN: Du är vid Storkyrkan. Om du tar den där gatan, Slotts-
                       backen, kommer du till Skeppsbrokajen. Gå till vänster
                       där och gå över Kungsträdgårdsgatan tills du kommer
                       till Hamngatan. På Hamngatan, sväng till höger och gå
                       ungefär två kvarter tills du kommer till Birger Jarls-
                       gatan. Sväng till vänster och gå ner Birger Jarlsgatan
                       förbi Stureplan och hotellet är på vänstra sidan.

Ms. LINDQUIST: Tack så mycket.

*Fru Lindquist går till hotellet. När hon äntligen kommer fram sover hon
middag, eftersom hon har gått så mycket.*

OLD MAN:	You are by *Storkyrkan* (the Great Church). If you take that street, The Castle Slope, you will come to Ships Bridge. Go left there and go over Royal Garden Street until you come to Harbor Street. At Harbor Street turn to the right and walk about two blocks until you come to Birger Jarl's Street. Turn left and walk down Birger Jarl's Street past Sture Square and the hotel will be on the left side.
MS. LINDQUIST:	Thank you very much.

Ms. Lindquist walks to her hotel. When she finally gets there she takes a nap because she has walked so much.

SAMTAL II

Efter att ha lämnat informationen i tågstationen, tycker Vince att han ska gå nerför Avenyn, en stor gata i Göteborg, men han har svårt att hitta vägen från tågstationen:

VINCE: Ursäkta mig, skulle du kunna hjälpa mig hitta Avenyn?

EN UNG KVINNA: Ja visst. Gå genom den här dörren bara och du är på Köpmansgatan. Gå till höger och förbi galleriet Nordstan. Då kommer du till en gata som heter Östra Hamngatan, gå till vänster och du är på Kungsportsavenyn, eller som vi säger, Avenyn, bara.

VINCE: Tack.

Vince vandrar upp för Avenyn tills han kommer till slutet, en plats som heter Götaplatsen. Han går på konstmuseet och tar ett glas vin på platsen. Han är nyfiken på ett ställe som heter Fiskekyrkan och vill titta på den men med alla krokiga gator har han gått vilse halva vägen ner för Avenyn:

VINCE: Ursäkta, jag försöker hitta Fiskekyrkan.

EN GAMMAL KVINNA: Tjaa, gå ner för Avenyn tills du går över Rosenlundskanalen. Då följer du kanalen, gatan byter namn några gånger men när den blir Rosenlundsgatan är du där. Men om du vill köpa goda fiskar kan jag föreslå Saluhallen. Stället heter också feskekörkan på Göteborgsdialekt.

VINCE: Tack.

Vince förstår inte kommentaren om att köpa fisk, men han följer hennes råd. När han kommer dit ser han att "Feskekörkan" är ett ställe att köpa fisk på. Han tycker att det är ett konstigt namn, men han får veta att det heter så för att utsidan av huset ser ut som en kyrka.

DIALOGUE II

After leaving the Information booth at the train station, Vince decides to walk down the Avenue, the main street in Gothenburg, but he has trouble finding his way from the train station:

VINCE: Excuse me, could you help me find The Avenue?

YOUNG WOMAN: Yes, of course. Just go out this door and you are on Merchant Street. Go to your right and pass the shopping mall Nordstan. You will come to a street called East Harbor Street, turn left and you are on The King's Port Avenue, or as we say, just The Avenue.

VINCE: Thanks.

Vince wanders up The Avenue until he comes to the end, a square called Goth Square. He goes into the Art Museum and has a glass of wine on the square. He is curious about a place called the Fish Church, and wants to see it, but with all the winding streets he finds himself lost halfway down The Avenue:

VINCE: Excuse me, I am trying to find the Fish Church.

OLD WOMAN: Well, go down The Avenue until you cross Rosenlund's canal. Then follow the canal, it will change names a couple times, but when it becomes Rosenlund's Street, you will be there. However, if you want good fish I recommend that you go to the Merchant Hall. And also it is called Fish Church, in the Gothenburg dialect.

VINCE: Thank you.

Vince does not understand the comment about buying fish, but he follows her advice. When he gets there, he sees that the Fish Church is a place to buy fish. He thinks it is a curious name, but learns that it is called that because the exterior of the building looks like a church.

VOCABULARY

Avenyn	aavehn**iw**n	The Avenue
bara *adv.*	b**aa**rah	only
beskriva i-e-e *v.*	behsk**ee**vah	describe
bro 2 *n. com.*	broo	bridge
byta IIb *v.*	b**iw**tah	change
dörr 2 *n. com.*	derrr	door
egen hand	**ay**gehn haand	on one's own
feskekörkan	fehskehsh**err**kahn	*see* Fiskekyrkan
fisk 2 *n. com.*	fisk	fish
Fiskekyrkan	fiskehsh**iw**rkahn	the Fish Church
fram *adv.*	frahm	forward
förbi *adv.*	ferrb**ee**	past
föreslå III *v.*	ferrehsl**oa**	suggest
förlåta IV å-ä-å *v.*	ferrl**oa**tah	try
förstå III *v.*	ferrst**oa**	understand
försöka IIb *v.*	ferrsh**er**kah	try
galleria 1 *n. com.*	gahllehr**ee**ah	a shopping mall
goda *adj. pl.*	g**oo**dah	good
gå vilse *v.*	goa v**i**lseh	get lost
gång 3 *n. com.*	gohng	time
gård 3 *n. com.*	gohrd	garden
halva *adj.*	h**ah**lvah	half
hjälpa IIb *v.*	**yeh**lpah	help
hur dags	hewr dahks	at what time
hus 5 *n. neu.*	hews	house
igen *adv.*	iy**eh**n	again
kanal 2 *n. com.*	kahn**ah**l	canal
kommentar 3 *n. com.*	kohmmehnt**aar**	comment
konstig *adj.*	k**oh**nstig	strange
krokig *adj.*	kr**oo**kig	winding
kunglig *adj.*	k**u**nglig	royal
kungsträdgården	kungstrehdg**oh**rdehn	royal gardens
konstmuseum	k**oh**nstmewsehum	art museum
kvarter 3 *n. com.*	kvahrt**ehr**	block/quarter

lämna I v.	lehmnah	leave
längs adv.	lehnks	along
meddela I v.	mayddehlah	inform
middag 2 n. com.	middah	afternoon
märka IIb v.	mehrkah	notice
nyfiken adj.	niwfeekehn	curious
nära adv.	naehrah	near
plats 3 n. com.	plahts	square/place
runt adv.	runt	around
råd n. neu.	road	advice
Saluhallen	saalewhahllehn	the Merchant Hall
se ut v.	say ewt	look like
sida 1 n. com.	seedah	side
slott 5 n. neu.	slohtt	castle
slut adj.	slewt	end
som conj.	sohm	as
stor adj.	stoor	big
ställa IIa v.	stehllah	place
svår adj.	svoar	difficult
så adv.	soa	so
tjaa intj.	chaah	well
två	tvoa	two
tågstation 3 n. com.	toagstahshoon	train station
ung adj.	ung	young
uppgift 3 n. com.	uppyift	information/ instructions
utsida 1 n. com.	ewtseedah	exterior
vaktombyte 4 n. neu.	vahktohmbiwteh	changing of the guards
vandra I v.	vahndrah	wander
vid prep.	veed	at
virrvarr 5 n. neu.	virrvahrr	muddle/confusion
väg 2 n. com.	vehg	way/road
äntligen adv.	ehntleegehn	finally
Östra adj.	erstrah	eastern

USEFUL EXPRESSIONS

Vad är det för hus?	What is that building?
När var det byggt?	When was it built?
Hur kommer jag till...?	How do I get to...?
bron	the bridge
affärskvarteret	the business district
kyrkogården	the cemetery
ambassaden	the embassy
fabriken	the factory
hamnen	the harbor
älven	the river
skeppskajen	the ship quay
universitetet	the university
Till vänster.	To the left.
Till höger.	To the right.
Rakt fram.	Straight ahead.
Jag har gått vilse.	I am lost.
Kan du visa mig vägen till...?	Can you show me the way to...?

GRAMMAR

1. Adverbs

Adverbs can be formed from most adjectives by using the neuter form of the adjective:

Huset är dåligt byggt.	*The house is badly built.*
Sov gott.	*Sleep well.*

Adjectives ending in -*lig* form adverbs by adding -*en* to the ending:

antagligen *probably*	troligen *probably*
egentligen *actually*	tydligen *evidently*
möjligen *possibly*	verkligen *really*

A few adjectives form their adverb counterparts with a -*vis* ending on the neuter form:

lyckligtvis *luckily*	naturligtvis *naturally*
möjligtvis *possibly*	troligtvis *probably*
vanligtvis *usually*	

Notice that some adverbs can be formed in both ways.

Many of the common adverbs are only adverbs:

nu *now*	igen *again*
in *in*	

These are but a few. The word *bra* can be used as either *well* or *good*.

2. Time adverbs

Below are some of the common adverbs denoting time:

aldrig *never*	alltid *always*
då *then*	då och då *now and then*
förr *before*	genast *at once*
ibland *sometimes*	länge *a long time*
nu *now*	nyss *just now*
någonsin *ever*	ofta *often*
redan *already*	sedan *then, afterward*
snart *soon*	strax *soon*
sällan *seldom*	ännu *still*

3. Directional adverbs

Swedish differentiates between direction and location adverbs. The adverbs in motion are used with motion verbs like *to go, to walk, to ride*, etc., whereas the adverbs at rest are used with *to be, to stay*, etc.:

AT REST	IN MOTION
borta *away*	bort *away*
där *there*	dit *there, thither*
framme *forward, up here*	fram *forward, up*
hemma *at home*	hem *home*
här *here*	hit *here, hither*
inne *in, inside*	in *in*
nere *down*	ner *down*
uppe *up*	upp *up*
ute *out*	ut *out*
var *where*	vart *where, whither*

A few examples may clarify this process:

Jag ska gå hem. *I am going home.*
Men du är hemma. *But you are home.*
Kom hit. *Come here.*
Jag är här. *I am here.*
Om du är ute, kom in. *If you are out(side), come in.*
Om du är inne, gå ut. *If you are in(side), go out.*

ÖVNINGAR

I. Skriv de följande adjektiven som adverb (Write the following adjectives as adverbs).

1. (konstig) _____.
2. (krokig) _____.
3. (svår) _____.
4. (snabb) _____.
5. (trevlig) _____.

II. Använd rätt ord (Use the right word).

1. (där/dit) Jag måste gå _____.
2. (ute/ut) Han är _____.
3. (hemma/hem) Hon kommer _____ snart.
4. (inne/in) Hon stannar _____ ikväll.
5. (uppe/upp) De kommer _____.
6. (var/vart) _____ är du nu?

III: Fyll i de rätta orden (Fill in the right words).

1. (never) Jag äter _____ fisk.
2. (then) Vi gick till affären _____.
3. (already) Jag förstår _____ svenska.
4. (ever) Har du _____ varit till Sverige?
5. (really) Åker du _____ till Stockholm?
6. (still) Jag förstår _____ inte.

IV. Översätt till svenska (Translate into Swedish).

1. I am lost.
2. Can you tell me how to get to the Royal Castle?
3. Is it far?
4. How do I get there?
5. I am trying to find the Fish Church.

V.   Översätt till engelska (Translate into English).

1. Det är nära kyrkan i Gamla Stan.
2. Gatan byter namn till Strömgatan.
3. Nu är du vid Storkyrkan.
4. Gå ut genom den här dörren bara och du är på Köpmansgatan.
5. Om du vill köpa god fisk kan jag föreslå Saluhallen.

ETYMOLOGY

There is a relationship between the Swedish -*lig* found at the end of adjectives and the English -*ly* found at the end of adverbs. As has often happened in old English, the *g* sound has changed in many words. The observant student of Swedish will notice many words in Swedish that retain that *g* sound, whereas they have been lost in English. Words such as *gul* in Swedish and *yellow* in English come from the same origins, yet the *g* in many words has changed to a *y*. This sound change has also happened in Swedish. Although Swedish retains the g in spelling, the sound of that letter in front of letters like *i*, *e*, *ä* and *ö* is often like a *y*.

Swedish retains some features of the language that are archaic in English. The word for why in Swedish, *varför*, will remind some students of their days studying Shakespeare. I remember as a high school student wondering why Juliette was asking herself where Romeo was in her famous soliloquy "Romeo, Romeo, wherefore art thou Romeo" when in fact she is asking why he is Romeo. In the past, some students have wondered why Swedish has two words for you, *du* and *ni*. Not only is *ni* plural, but it is also the old formal form, which is having something of a comeback these days. The word *ni* is actually formed from a misunderstanding. The word used to be *I*. This older form had its own conjugation, which is never used today, that is formed with an *n*, thus *I haven* (you have). Since Swedish regularly places the subject after the verb, the word order was often *haven I*, and thereby became *have ni*. If that seems strange, remember that in English *an apron* used to be *a napron*. This *du* and *I* form in Swedish has its cognates in English *thou* and *ye* respectively. However, in English we have retained the formal form, *you*, and abandoned the familiar form, *thou*.

Another feature in Swedish that students may remember from their Shakespeare days are adverbs of motion like *hither*, *thither*, and *whither* or *to here*, *to there*, and *to where*. Though we in English no longer use those adverbs of motion, in Swedish they are still very much alive in the forms *hit*, *dit*, and *vart*.

Business and Economics

The major industries in Sweden are construction, engineering, mining, steel, motor vehicles, telecommunications and information technology, forestry, and agriculture.

Steel is amongst the oldest industries in Sweden and dates back to the thirteenth century. In 1970s the steel industry represented 50% of the labor force. Today that number is much less, as only about 4% of industrial labor works in the steel industry. Nevertheless it is still an important industry for Sweden. In 1997 it represented 14 billion Swedish kronor, or 1.75 billion dollars, in export revenue. As a comparison, the United States imported over 2.5 billion dollars in alloy exchange stainless, stainless, and ordinary steel that year.

Automobile manufacturing is another important industry for Sweden. In 1998 the collective revenues for Volvo, Saab Automobile, and Scania was 286 billion Swedish kronor, or around 36 billion dollars. One of every 10 manufacture workers in Sweden works for the automobile or automobile parts industry and 9 out of 10 automobiles manufactured are exports. In 1997 the automobile industry in cars and parts exported 81 billion Swedish kronor, or 10 billion dollars, which was 13% of the total exports. Though Swedish automobile manufacturing accounts for a mere 1% of the total automobile manufacturing in the world, Sweden is one of the largest manufacturers of heavy trucks over 16 tons. One-fifth of all heavy truck manufacturing in 1998 was done by Volvo or Scania.

Sweden is a leader in information technology. It ranks second, after the United States. Over 50% of the public regularly surfs the Net and Sweden is wiring the country to promote greater access and faster connection speeds. One of the major manufacturers of cell phones is Eriksson, who in 1999 reported a net earning of 215 billion Swedish kronor, or 27 billion dollars, and has operations in more than 130 countries with 100,000 employees.

The forest industry is another very old industry in Sweden. In 1997 Sweden produced 10 million metric tons of wood and paper products. In 1996 the forest industry represented 3.7% of the Gross Domestic Product of Sweden. While exporting 631 billion Swedish kronor (79 billion dollars) in wood and paper products, Sweden also imported 499 billion Swedish kronor (62 billion dollars).

Sweden is one of largest countries in Europe, a little larger than the state of California. One half the country is covered by forest, and one third by mountains, lakes, and marshes. One tenth of the area is cultivated. Nevertheless, agriculture remains an important industry. In 1996, Sweden exported approximately 15 billion Swedish kronor, 2 billion dollars, in foodstuffs. That same year Swedish imports were 33 billion, or 4 billion dollars.

LESSON
6

SAMTAL I

Att handla.

Fru Lindquist vill gå ut och handla. Herr Anderssons syster, Monika Andersson, tar henne till några affärer i Stockholms centrum:

FRU ANDERSSON: Tycker fru Lindquist om Sverige?

FRU LINDQUIST: Du kan kalla mig för Donna. Ja, Jag tycker mycket om Sverige. Det finns så mycket att se här, så mycket historia.

FRU ANDERSSON: Jag är glad att du tycker om det. Vad vill du handla?

FRU LINDQUIST: Jag skulle helst hitta lite svenskt glas. Och kanske någonting åt min mor, kanske en tröja.

FRU ANDERSSON: Jag vet vart vi kan gå för att hitta dem.

Fru Andersson och fru Lindquist går till NK, ett stort varuhus på Hamngatan:

FRU LINDQUIST: O, titta! Där finns det några svenska tröjor. Jag skulle helst köpa en åt min mor. (*Till expediten*) Hur mycket kostar den blåa tröjan?

EXPEDITEN: Den kostar etttusenfemhundra kronor.

FRU LINDQUIST: Den är lite för dyr. Har du någon lite billigare?

EXPEDITEN: De här kostar bara sjuhundrafemtio kronor. Det är rea idag.

FRU LINDQUIST: O vad trevligt! Har du en liten? Min mor är väldigt liten.

DIALOGUE I

Shopping.

Ms. Lindquist wants to go shopping. Mr. Andersson's sister, Monika Andersson, is going to take her to several shops in downtown Stockholm:

MS. ANDERSSON: Do you like Sweden, Ms. Lindquist?

MS. LINDQUIST: You can call me Donna. Yes, I have enjoyed Sweden very much. There is so much to see here and so much history.

MS. ANDERSSON: I am glad you are enjoying it. What would you like to shop for?

MS. LINDQUIST: I would love to find some of the Swedish glass. And perhaps something for my mother, a sweater maybe.

MS. ANDERSSON: I know just where to go to find those.

Ms. Andersson and Ms. Lindquist walk to NK, a big department store on Harbor Street:

MS. LINDQUIST: Oh, look, there are some of the Swedish sweaters. I would like to buy one for my mother. (*To the clerk*) How much is that blue sweater?

CLERK: That one is 1,500 crowns.

MS. LINDQUIST: It's a little too expensive. Do you have any a little cheaper?

CLERK: These here are only 750 crowns. There is a sale today.

MS. LINDQUIST: Oh that is nice! Do you have a small one? My mother is quite small.

EXPEDITEN: Ja, skulle den här passa?

FRU LINDQUIST: O ja! Den är mycket bra. Tar du kreditkort?

EXPEDITEN: Naturligtvis.

FRU LINDQUIST: Då tar jag den.

Efter att ha betalat för tröjan tittar fru Lindquist och fru Andersson på svenskt glas:

FRU LINDQUIST: Vad vackert glaset är! Jag älskar svenskt glas.

FRU ANDERSSON: Det där är gjort på det svenska glasbruket Orrefors.

FRU LINDQUIST: Det är verkligen vackert. Jag tror att jag tar den här glas-satsen.

FRU ANDERSSON: Det blir kanske svårt att få hem dem på planet.

EXPEDITEN: Vi kan skicka dem till dig. Vi drar bort skatten, vilket betalar nästan hela frakten och försäkringen.

FRU LINDQUIST: Det är fint, då är de där när jag kommer hem. Jag tar dem.

CLERK:　　　　Yes, would this be good?

MS. LINDQUIST:　Oh yes! That is very good. Will you take a credit card?

CLERK:　　　　Naturally.

MS. LINDQUIST:　Then I'll take it.

After paying for the sweater, Ms. Lindquist and Ms. Andersson look for Swedish glass:

MS. LINDQUIST:　How beautiful the crystal is! I love Swedish glass.

MS. ANDERSSON:　This one is made at the Swedish glassworks Orrefors.

MS. LINDQUIST:　It is quite lovely. I think I will take this set of glasses.

MS. ANDERSSON:　It may be hard to get them home on the plane.

CLERK:　　　　We can ship them to you. We take off the taxes, which almost pays for the shipping and insurance.

MS. LINDQUIST:　That's great, then they will be there when I come home. I'll take them.

SAMTAL II

Vince är ute på egen hand på Avenyn. Han letar efter ett par nya skor:

VINCE: Jag skulle vilja köpa ett par nya skor.

EXPEDITEN: Vilken färg?

VINCE: Bruna.

EXPEDITEN: Vilken storlek har du?

VINCE: Fyrtiofem, tror jag.

EXPEDITEN: Prova de här.

VINCE: De är lite för stora. Istället provar jag fyrtiofyra.

EXPEDITEN: Bra. Jag har de här i fyrtiofyra också. Här. Prova de här. Passar de?

VINCE: Ja. De är vackra. Och de passar bra också. Hur mycket kostar de?

EXPEDITEN: Etttusensjuhundra kronor.

VINCE: Oj då, det var dyrt. Har du några som är lite billigare?

EXPEDITEN: Låt mig tänka. Ett ögonblick. Jag hämtar dem. Varsågod. De här kostar bara sexhundrafemtio.

VINCE: De här är inte lika bra som de där, men de är bra. Låt mig prova dem. *(När han har provat dem)* Jo, jag tycker om de här. Jag köper dem. Jag skulle också vilja köpa ett par träskor.

EXPEDITEN: De kostar fyrahundra kronor.

VINCE: Bra, jag tar dem också.

DIALOGUE II

Vince is out on his own on Avenyn. He wants to find a new pair of shoes:

VINCE: I would like to buy a new pair of shoes.

CLERK: What color?

VINCE: Brown.

CLERK: What size do you wear?

VINCE: I think 45.

CLERK: Try these on.

VINCE: They are too big. Perhaps I should try a 44.

CLERK: Ok, I have these in 44 also. Here try these. Do they fit?

VINCE: Yes they are beautiful. And they fit well too. How much do they cost?

CLERK: One thousand seven hundred crowns.

VINCE: Oh, too expensive. Do you have anything a little cheaper?

CLERK: Let me think. One moment, I'll get them. Here you are. These are only 650.

VINCE: These are not as nice as those, but they are nice. Let me try them on. (*After trying them on*) Yes, I like these. I will buy them. I would also like a pair of clogs.

CLERK: They are 400 crowns.

VINCE: Ok, I'll take them too.

VOCABULARY

betala I *v.*	beht**ah**lah	pay
billigare *adj.*	b**i**lleegahreh	cheaper
bort *adv.*	bohrt	away
brun *adj.*	brewn	brown
egen *adj.*	**ay**gehn	own
expedit 3 *n. com.*	ehkspehd**eet**	sales clerk
fler *adj.*	flayr	many
frakt 3 *n. com.*	frahkt	postage
färg 2 *n. com.*	f**eh**ry	color
för *adv.*	ferr	too
försäkring 2 *n. com.*	ferrsh**eh**kreeng	insurance
glad *adj.*	glaad	glad
glassats 3 *n. com.*	gl**aa**ssahts	set of glasses
glasbruk 5 *n. neu.*	gl**aa**sbrewk	glassworks
hand (*pl.* händer) *n. com.*	hahnd	hand
handla I *v.*	h**ah**ndlah	shop
hel *adj.*	hayl	whole
helst *adv.*	hehlst	preferably
historia 1 *n. com.*	hist**oo**reeah	history
hämta I *v.*	h**eh**mtah	fetch
istället *adv.*	eest**eh**lleht	instead
kalla I *v.*	k**ah**llah	call
kosta I *v.*	k**oh**stah	cost
kreditkort 4 *n. neu.*	krehd**eet**kohrt	credit card
leta efter I *v.*	l**ay**tah **eh**ftehr	search for
lik *adj.*	leek	like/similar
liten (litet-små) *adj.*	l**ee**tehn	little
mindre *adj.*	m**i**ndreh	smaller
mor (*pl.* mödrar) *n. com.*	moor	mother
naturligtvis *adv.*	naht**ewr**litvees	naturally
NK	**eh**nkoh	a department store
nästan *adv.*	n**eh**staan	almost
Orrefors	err**eh**fohrsh	Swedish glassworks
par 5 *n. neu.*	paar	pair

passa I v.	pahssah	suit
plan 5 n. neu.	plaahn	level
prova I v.	proovah	try out/on
rea 1 n. com.	rayah	sale
se (ser-såg-sett) v.	say	see
skatt 3 n. neu.	skahtt	tax
skicka I v.	shikkah	send
sko (pl. skor) n. com.	skoo	shoe
skulle v.	skulleh	would/should
som pron.	sohm	who
som conj.	sohm	as
storlek 2 n. com.	stoorlehk	size
syster (pl. systrar) n. com.	siwstehr	sister
titta I v.	tittah	look
tro III v.	troo	believe
träskor n. com.	trayskoor	clogs
tröja 1 n. com.	treryah	sweater
tycka IIb v.	tikkah	believe
vad intj.	vah	how! what!
vacker adj.	vahkehr	beautiful
vart adv.	vahrt	where to
varuhus n. neu.	vaarewhews	department store
verkligen adv.	vehrkleegen	really
veta V (vet-visste-vetat) v.	vaytah	know
vilken pron.	vilkehn	which
väldig adj.	vehldeeg	huge
älska I v.	ehlskah	love
än conj.	ehn	than (with comparisons)
ögonblick 5 n. neu.	ergohnblikk	moment

USEFUL EXPRESSIONS

Var kan jag hitta...?	Where can I find...?
Var säljer man...?	Where do they sell...?
Kan du hjälpa mig?	Can you help me?
Kan du visa mig...?	Can you show me...?
ett skärp	a belt
en blus	a blouse
en mössa	a cap
en kappa	a coat
en klänning	a dress
en päls	a fur coat
ett par jeans	a pair of jeans
ett par byxor	a pair of pants
ett par skor	a pair of shoes
ett par strumpor	a pair of socks
en kjol	a skirt
en tröja	a sweater
en väst	a vest
Jag vill ha en som är ...	I want one that is ...
svart	black
blå	blue
brun	brown
grå	gray
grön	green
brandgul	orange
rosa	pink
lila	purple
röd	red
vit	white
gul	yellow
större	bigger
mindre	smaller
smalare	narrower
bredare	wider

<u>SIZES</u>

DRESSES

American	6	8	10	12	14	16	18	20
Swedish	34	36	38	40	42	44	46	48

MEN'S COATS

American	32	34	36	38	40	42	44	46
Swedish	42	44	46	48	50	52	54	56

WOMEN'S SHOES

American	6	7	8	9	10	11
Swedish	37	38	40	41	43	44

MEN'S SHOES

American	6	7	8	9	10	11
Swedish	39	41	42	43	44	45

GRAMMAR

1. Adjectives II: comparatives and superlatives

The comparative has only one form, which is used for common (*en*-nouns), neuter (*ett*-nouns), plural, definite, and indefinite nouns. Most comparatives are formed in Swedish by adding *-are*, like the English *-er*. Most superlatives have two forms, one used for common and neuter indefinite nouns, *-ast*, and another used for plural and definite nouns, *-aste*:

BASE	COM.	SUP.	SUP. DEF.
fri *free*	friare	friast	friaste
hård *hard*	hårdare	hårdast	hårdaste
röd *red*	rödare	rödast	rödaste
stark *strong*	starkare	starkast	starkaste

Adjectives that end in *-er*, *-el*, or *-en* lose the *-e-* in the stem of the word as was seen with plural adjectives:

BASE	COM.	SUP.	SUP. DEF.
enkel *simple*	enklare	enklast	enklaste
mogen *mature*	mognare	mognast	mognaste
vacker *beautiful*	vackrare	vackrast	vackraste

A few adjectives do not have an *-a* in either the comparative or superlative forms and sometimes undergo a vowel shift in the stem of the word. In the superlative, those adjectives not having an *-a* have a *-sta* ending in the definite:

BASE	COM.	SUP.	SUP. DEF.
grov *coarse*	grövre	grövst	grövsta
hög *high*	högre	högst	högsta
låg *low*	lägre	lägst	lägsta
lång *long*	längre	längst	längsta

stor *big*	större	störst	största
trång *narrow*	trängre	trängst	trängsta
tung *heavy*	tyngre	tyngst	tyngsta
ung *young*	yngre	yngst	yngsta

And, like English, there are a few irregular adjectives:

BASE	COM.	SUP.	SUP. DEF.
bra *good*	bättre	bäst	bästa
dålig *bad*	sämre	sämst	sämsta
dålig *evil*	värre	värst	värsta
gammal *old*	äldre	äldst	äldsta
god *good*	bättre	bäst	bästa
liten *small*	mindre	minst	minsta
många *many*	fler(a)	flest	flesta

As in English there are a few adjectives that cannot take an ending in the comparative and superlative and therefore must be formed with *mer* and *mest*. This applies mostly to adjectives ending in -*isk* and all participles used as adjectives:

| energisk *energetic* | mer energisk | mest energisk | den mest energiska |
| irriterad *irritated* | mer irriterad | mest irriterad | den mest irriterade |

Finally, an equalizing comparison is formed in the following way:

Han är **lika** stor **som** jag. *He is as big as I.*

A comparison is expressed like this:

Han är större **än** hon. *He is bigger than she.*

And a negative comparison is expressed like this:

Det är inte **så** stor **som** jag trodde. *It is not as big as I thought.*

2. tycka - tänka - tro

One issue that often trips up students is the use of the verbs *tycka*, *tänka*, and *tro*. Though they can seem at times to mean the same thing, *think*, they are used in differing circumstances. The verb *tycka* often carries with it the idea of desire or opinion, e.g. *vad tycker du om filmen?*—what did you think about the film? The verb *tänka* is the actual process of thinking, as in *han tänker hårt just nu* —he is thinking hard right now. Whereas *tro* is best described as believing, as with *jag tror det*—I think so.

3. kunna - veta - känna

Another pair of words that causes students pause are *kan* and *vet*. The verb *kan* often means *can* or *to be able to*, but it also can mean *know*. When used as *know*, *kan* is the knowing of how to do something, as in *kan du svenska?*— do you know Swedish? or *kan du fysik?*—do you know physics? The verb *vet* is used for facts that you can know, as in *vet du vad han heter?*—do you know what his name is?, or *vet du vad vi ska ha till middag idag?*—do you know what we are having for dinner tonight? The verb *känner* is only used for people, as in *känner du hennes mor?*—do you know her mother?

ÖVNINGAR

I. Skriv de följande adjektiven som komparativ och översätt till engelska
    (Write the following adjectives as comparatives and translate to English).

    1. (konstig) Han är _____ än jag.
    2. (stor) Min väska är _____ än din väska.
    3. (lätt) Svenska är _____ än jag trodde.
    4. (snabb) Du är snabb men hon är_____.
    5. (ung) Han är _____ än du.

II. Fyll i den rätta formen (Use the right words).

    1. Jag är stark men du är _____. Hon är den _____av oss
       alla.
    2. Jag är dålig och han är _____ än henne, men det där barnet är det
       _____barnet jag känner.
    3. Du är mogen och hon är _____ än du, men han är den
       _____.
    4. (enkel) De här övningarna är de _____ jag har gjort.
    5. Jag trodde jag var irriterad men han var _____ och hon var
       den _____ jag har sett.

III. Fyll i de rätta orden *tycka - tänka - tro* (Fill in the right words).

    1. Jag _____ att svenska är kul.
    2. _____ du på vad jag säger?
    3. Jag _____ att jag ska åka till Sverige.
    4. _____ hårt.
    5. _____ om vi skulle kunna åka dit.
    6. _____ du att du kanske ska komma till Sverige?

IV. Fyll i de rätta orden *kunna - veta - känna* (Fill in the right words).

    1. Jag _____ svenska nu!
    2. _____ du hur man säger det?

3. Jag _____ inte dig.
4. _____ du henne?
5. Jag _____ inte engelska.
6. Jag _____ hur gammal du är.

V.   Översätt till svenska (Translate into Swedish).

1. There is so much to see here.
2. I would like to buy a pair of shoes.
3. It is too expensive. Do you have anything cheaper.
4. I would like to try this sweater on.
5. I like this one. I would like to buy it.

VI.   Översätt till engelska (Translate into English).

1. Tycker du om Sverige?
2. Vad vill du handla?
3. Det finns tröjor i den affären.
4. Passar de?
5. Vilken storlek har du?

ETYMOLOGY

Swedish and English are related languages and it has only been a thousand years since they were mutually intelligible. There are many words that are still recognizable to the English speaker. The colors are one such group of words that are very similar. It is not impossible for an English speaker to understand words like *blå, brun, grön, grå, röd,* and *vit* (blue, brown, green, grey, red, and white respectively). It may be a little harder to recognize that *gul* is related to yellow, but as one knows that a *g* in Swedish is often a *y* in English, that too may be discernable.

The odd word out, as it were, is the word *svart,* in English black. As it happens, English is the odd language out as far as the Germanic languages are concerned. Through a strange set of circumstances, our word *black* is actually related to the Romance word for *white,* for example the French *blanc* or the Spanish *blanco,* which was the ancient word for ash or something having been burned. As anyone who has seen ash in a campfire can tell you, sometimes the ash is white, and sometimes it is black.

Art and Culture

Despite being a small nation of only nine million people, Sweden is rich in art and culture. Sweden also spends a lot of public money in order to promote culture and the arts. In 1974 parliament voted unanimously for a state cultural policy. Between the time this act was adopted and 1984 the state's contribution more than doubled. In 1996 Swedes spent 43.75 billion kronor, or 5.5 billion dollars, on culture including theater and dance, music, literature libraries, museums and exhibitions, films and cinemas, popular education, and daily press periodicals to name but a few. Households and consumers paid 65% of the cost.

In the last century and a half Sweden has seen a number of world class authors. There are naturally too many authors for this short overview, but here are perhaps just a few of the better known. Selma Lagerlöf (1858–1940) captured the imagination of readers with *Gösta Berling's Saga* (1891), and became the first woman to win the Nobel Prize in 1909. Pär Lagerkvist (1891–1974) was an early pioneer of Swedish modernism, who examined the relationship between God and man in such novels as *Barrabas* (1950) and *The Sibyl* (1956). Lagerkvist also received the Nobel Prize in 1951. Vilhelm Moberg (1898–1973) has penned the classic epic of Swedish immigration to America, *The Emigrants* (1949), *The Immigrants* (1952), *Unto a Good Land* (1956), and *Last Letter Home* (1959). Ivar Lo-Johansson's (1901–1990) novel, *Breaking Free* (1933) presents a moving account of the conditions that caused many Swedes to emigrate. Sara Lidman (b. 1923) became an overnight success with the novel *The Tar Pit* (1953), which she wrote in dialect and discusses the plight of the small farmers of Northern Sweden. Per Christian Jersild (b. 1935), a medical doctor with a calling to write, has produced several novels that deal with the central ethical issues of technology and modern life, such as *A Living Soul* (1980) and *The Animal Doctor* (1973). Finally, Kerstin Ekman (b. 1933) had considerable success in the United States with her literate mystery novel, *Blackwater* (1993).

August Strindberg (1849–1912) is one of the world's great dramatists, and perhaps Sweden's most controversial and innovative author. His influence can be felt in the work of Tennesee Williams, Eugene O'Neill, and even surreal videos on MTV. Although he wrote for the stage, perhaps his legacy is one of the reasons that Swedish film has maintained such a high standard throughout the twentieth century. In the early part of the century, Stockholm vied with Hollywood and Berlin for cinematic preeminence. Greta Gustafsson, later called Greta Garbo, was one of the figures of this early film industry. Over the years, the Swedes have produced a number of fine actors and actresses who have also found success in Hollywood, such as Ingrid Bergman, Max von Sydow, Stellan Skarsgård, Lena Olin, and Peter Stormare. Ingmar Bergman was a keen student of Strindberg's work, and has been one of the most influential filmmakers of the twentieth century. Bergman's extensive catalogue of films from *Wild Strawberries* (1957) to *Fanny and Alexander* (1982) have brought him international fame. Director Lasse Hallström garnered international acclaim for his moving film, *My Life as a Dog* (1985). The success of that film has led to further successes in Hollywood, such as *The Cider House Rules* (1999) and *Chocolat* (2000).

The Swedish government endeavors to support and create job opportunities for artists by expanding cultural institutions, supporting independent groups and cultural centers as well as purchasing artists' works for public viewing and public buildings. In 2000, the Swedish Art Council had a budget of 31 million kronor, 4 million dollars, in order to support the visual arts and artists.

LESSON
7

SAMTAL I

Vänner.

Fru Lindquist är bjuden hem till Herr Andersson på middag. Sex medarbetare är också bjudna på middag. Fru Lindquist är fem minuter försenad och alla andra gäster har redan kommit:

HERR ANDERSSON: Välkommen. Stig på. Får jag ta din rock?

FRU LINDQUIST: Ja tack. Är jag sist? Förlåt att jag är försenad.

HERR ANDERSSON: Fem minuter bara. Jo, de andra är här. (*Herr Andersson ler*) Ingen kommer för sent i Sverige. Fru Lindquist, jag skulle vilja presentera dig för Pär Berg och jag tror att du känner de andra från kontoret.

PÄR BERG: Trevligt att träffas.

HERR ANDERSSON: Skulle damen vilja ha en välkomstdrink?

FRU LINDQUIST: Ja tack, gärna.

Herr Andersson ger Fru Lindquist ett litet glas:

HERR ANDERSSON: Skål och välkomna!

EVERYONE: Skål!

Alla pratar i några minuter och sedan kallas de till bords där ett namnkort har ställts för varje gäst. Fru Lindquist är placerad brevid herr Berg.

DIALOGUE I

Friends.

Ms. Lindquist is invited to Mr. Andersson's house for dinner. Six other co-workers are also invited to dinner. Ms. Lindquist arrives five minutes late and all the other guests have already arrived:

MR. ANDERSSON: Welcome. Come in. Can I take your coat?

MS. LINDQUIST: Yes, thank you. Am I the last one? Sorry I am late.

MR. ANDERSSON: Only five minutes. Yes, the others are here. *(Mr. Andersson smiles)* No one comes too late in Sweden. Ms. Lindquist, I would like to introduce you to Pär Berg and I think you know the others from the office.

PÄR BERG: Pleased to meet you.

MR. ANDERSSON: Would you like a little welcome drink?

MS. LINDQUIST: Yes, thank you very much.

Mr. Andersson gives Ms. Lindquist a small glass:

MR. ANDERSSON: Cheers and welcome!

EVERYONE: Cheers!

All guests talk for a few minutes, then they are called to the table where a name card has been placed for each of the guests. Ms. Lindquist finds herself next to Mr. Berg.

SAMTAL II

Vince har varit i Sverige i en vecka och vill ringa en kompis för att kolla saker hemma. Han frågar Eva om bästa sättet att göra det på:

VINCE: Jag vill ringa min kompis för att kolla om allt är bra hemma. Vad är bästa sättet att göra det på?

EVA: Det är förmodligen bäst att köpa ett telefonkort och ringa från en Telia telefonautomat. Du kan köpa ett i kiosken där borta.

Vince köper ett telefonkort. Han går till en telefon och Eva hjälper honom. Han pratar med sin kompis tills tiominuters kortet tar slut.

EVA: Skulle du vilja fika?

VINCE: Ja, skulle vi kunna gå tillbaka till kiosken först så att jag kan köpa några vykort att skicka hem?

EVA: Visst.

Vid kaffet skriver Vince sina vykort och pratar med Eva:

VINCE: Kan du säga mig var posten ligger?

EVA: Visst. Det är inte långt dit. Det är till vänster och ungefär en kvarter rakt fram. Men du kan köpa frimärken i samma kiosk och lägga dina vykort i postlådan.

VINCE: Tack så mycket.

Vince köper sina frimärken i kiosken och stoppar sina vykort i postlådan:

VINCE: Låt oss gå på ett internetkafé, då kan jag skicka e-post till min kompis.

EVA: Okej, de där ställena är kul i alla fall, men de kan vara dyra.

Eva och Vince slösar bort eftermiddagen genom att surfa nätet.

DIALOGUE II

Vince has been in Sweden for a week and wants to call his friend to check on things at home. He asks Eva the best way to do this.

VINCE: I want to call my friend to check if everything is ok at home. What is the best way to do this?

EVA: It's probably best to buy a telephone card and call from a Telia pay phone. You can buy one from that stand over there.

Vince buys a telephone card. He goes to a telephone and Eva helps him. He talks with his friend until the 10-minute telephone card runs out.

EVA: Would you like to get a cup of coffee?

VINCE: Yes, could we go back to that stand first, so I can buy some postcards to send home?

EVA: Sure.

Over coffee, Vince writes his postcards and talks with Eva:

VINCE: Can you tell me where the post office is?

EVA: Sure. It's not far. It is to the left and about a block down. But you can buy stamps at that same stand and put your cards in the mailbox.

VINCE: Thanks a lot.

Vince buys his stamps at the stand and stuffs his cards in the mailbox:

VINCE: Let's go into this cyber café and I can send an e-mail to a friend of mine.

EVA: Ok, those places are fun anyway, but they can be expensive.

Eva and Vince kill the afternoon by surfing on the Internet.

VOCABULARY

automat 3 *n. com.*	aaewtohm**aa**t	automat
bjuden *adj.*	by**we**dehn	invited
bredvid *prep.*	brehv**ee**d	next to
dam 2 *n. com.*	d**aa**m	lady
eftermiddag 2 *n. com.*	ehftehrm**i**ddah	afternoon
e-post 3 *n. com.*	**ay**pohst	e-mail
fika I *v.*	f**ee**kah	have coffee
frimärke 4 *n. neu.*	fr**ee**mehrkeh	stamp
förmodligen *adv.*	furrm**oh**dleegehn	probably
gäst 3 *n. com.*	y**e**hst	guest
i alla fall *adv.*	ee **ah**llah fahll	anyway
ingen *pro.*	**i**ngehn	no one
kiosk 2 *n. com.*	sh**ee**ohsk	stand/booth
kolla I *v.*	k**oh**llah	check
kompis 2 *n. com.*	k**oh**mpees	friend
le (ler-log-lett) *v.*	l**ay**	smile
lägga V	l**eh**ggah	put/lay
(lägger-la(de)-lagt) *v.*		
medarbetare	m**ay**dahrbehtahreh	co-worker
(*pl.* -are) *n. com.*		
middag 2 *n. com.*	m**i**ddah	dinner
namnkort 5 *n. neu.*	n**ah**mnkohrt	name card
nät 5 *n. neu.*	n**e**ht	Internet/Net
placerad *adj.*	pl**aa**sehrahd	placed
post 3 *n. com.*	p**oh**st	mail
postlåda *n. com.*	p**oh**stloadah	mailbox
prata I *v.*	pr**aa**tah	talk
presentera I *v.*	prehsehnt**ay**rah	present
rock 2 *n. com.*	r**oh**kk	coat
rakt *adv.*	r**aa**kt	straight
redan *adv.*	r**ay**dahn	already
sak 3 *n. com.*	s**aa**k	thing
samma *adj.*	s**ah**mmah	same
sedan *adv.*	s**ay**dahn *or* sehn	then

sig *pro.*	say	himself/herself
sin *pro.*	seen	his/her own
sist *adj.*	sist	last
skriva IV i-e-i *v.*	skreevah	write
skål *intj.*	skoal	cheers
sluta I *v.*	slewtah	stop/finish
slösa I *v.*	slursah	while away/waste
stoppa I *v.*	stohppah	put/stuff
surfa I *v.*	surfah	surf
sätt 5 *n. neu.*	sehtt	way/manner
telefonkort 5 *n. neu.*	tehlehfohnkohrt	telephone card
Telia	tehleeah	the phone company
till bords	till bohrds	to the table
varje *adj.*	vahryeh	each
vykort 5 *n. neu.*	viwkohrt	postcard
välkomst 3 *n. com.*	vaylkohmst	welcome

USEFUL EXPRESSIONS

Var ligger postkontoret?	Where is the post office?
Var kan jag köpa frimärken?	Where can I buy stamps?
Vad kostar ett vykort till USA?	What does it cost for a postcard to the US?
Vad kostar ett brev till USA?	What does it cost for a letter to the US?
Var kan jag köpa en tidning?	Where can I buy a newspaper?
Hur länge har du varit här?	How long have you been here?
Reser du ensam?	Are you traveling alone?
Jag är med ...	I'm with ...
min man	my husband
min fru	my wife
min familj	my family
mina föräldrar	my parents
min syster	my sister
min bror	my brother
mina vänner	my friends

Jag skulle vilja bjuda dig på middag.	I would like to invite you to dinner.
Kan du komma över på en drink?	Can you join us for a drink?
Det är en fest.	There is a party.
Hur dags ska jag komma?	What time should I come?
Tack för ikväll. Det var fint.	Thanks for the evening, it was great.

frukost	breakfast
lunch	lunch
middag	dinner

GRAMMAR

1. Prepositions

Prepositions are the most difficult part of any language and ultimately must be learned as one goes. Below, however, are some rough guides that may aid the student through the quagmire of prepositions.

This is a list of all Swedish prepositions and their approximate meaning with a few examples. It cannot be stressed enough, however, that prepositions are best learned through memorizing them in their specific context:

av	by/of
Boken är av Strindberg.	*The book is by Strindberg.*

*Note: phrases like *king of Sweden* are almost always phrased in Swedish *Sveriges kung.*

efter	after
Vi dricker kaffe efter middagen.	*We drink coffee after dinner.*
emot	against
Han är emot den nya skatten.	*He is against the new tax.*
framför	in front of
Hon är framför mig.	*She is in front of me.*
från	from
Är ni från Wisconsin?	*Are you from Wisconsin?*
för	for/to/of
Det var bra för fisk.	*It was good for fish.*
Han är rädd för barn.	*He is afraid of children.*
Eva presenteras för Vince.	*Eva is introduced to Vince.*

för ____sedan	____ ago
Vi var där för tre veckor sedan.	*We were there three weeks ago.*
genom	through
Gå genom dörren.	*Go through the door.*
hos	at
Jag är hemma hos en kompis.	*I am at a friend's house.*
i	in
Jag är i Sverige nu!	*I am in Sweden now!*
but Jag talar i telefon.	*I am talking on the telephone.*
ifrån	from
Vi kommer ifrån USA.	*We come from the US.*

Note: the primary difference between *från* and *ifrån* is one of emphasis on the preposition. Also phrases like *from here* or *from there* and *from where* are expressed in Swedish as *härifrån*, *därifrån*, and *varifrån*.

igenom	through
Har du gått igenom	*Have you gone through your*
dina övningar?	*exercises?*

Note: like *ifrån* and *från*, the primary difference between *genom* and *igenom* is one of emphasis.

med	with
Hon är med oss.	*She is with us.*
mot	towards/against
Den här bussen går mot stan.	*This bus goes towards the city.*
Han luter mot väggen.	*He leaning against the window.*
om	about
Hon pratar om dig.	*She is talking about you.*

på	on/in/at
Glaset är på bordet.	*The glass is on the table.*
Vi sitter på vår plats.	*We are sitting in our places.*
Han är på kontoret.	*He is at the office.*

till	to
Matt vill resa till Sverige.	*Matt wants to travel to Sweden.*

under	under
Barnet sitter under bordet.	*The child is sitting under the table.*

vid	at/by/next to
Eva träffar Vince vid tågstationen.	*Eva meets Vince at the train station.*
Han är vid affären.	*He is by the store.*

åt	in/towards/for
Han går åt det hållet.	*He is walking in that direction.*
Eva köper en tröja åt Vince.	*Eva buys a sweater for Vince.*

över	over
Jag är glad att det är över.	*I am glad that it is over.*

1.1 PREPOSITIONS: TIME

Prepositions of time require their own explanation. Below are common time phrases and their Swedish counterparts:

for a week	i en vecka
in a week	om en vecka
during the day	under dagen
after dinner	efter middagen
a week ago	för en vecka sedan
last spring	i våras
last winter	i vintras
last summer	i somras
last fall	i höstas

day before yesterday	i förrgår
yesterday	igår
today	idag
tomorrow	imorgon
day after tomorrow	i övermorgon
last night	i natt
this morning	i morse
this afternoon	i eftermiddag
this evening	i kväll
tonight	i natt
last Monday	i måndags
last Tuesday	i tisdags
this spring	i vår
this winter	i vinter
once a day	en gång om dagen
one more time	en gång till
five to six	fem i sex
five after six	fem över sex

Note that there is a difference in Swedish between *gång* and *tid*, both of which translate into *time* in English. If you can count the number of times, the word used is *gång*, as in hur många gånger har du varit i Sverige— *how many times have you been to Sweden*. If it is abstract and cannot be made plural in English, the word to use is *tid*, as inhar du tid nu—*do you have time now*.

2.   *sin-sitt-sina-sig*

The word *sin* is a reflexive pronoun and is used only when the thing owned belongs to the subject of the sentence and when the subject of the sentence is third person:

    Han har sitt glas. *He has his (own) glass.*
but Han har hans glas. *He has his (someone else's) glass.*

    Erik har sin bok. *Erik has his (own) book.*
but Erik har hans bok. *Erik has his (someone else's) book.*

Hon skrev ett brev till sin man. *She wrote a letter to her (own) husband.*

but: Hon skrev ett brev till hennes man. *She wrote a letter to her (someone else's) husband.*

Eva läser ett brev från sin man. *Eva reads a letter from her (own) husband.*

but: Eva läser ett brev från hennes man. *Eva reads a letter from her (someone else's) husband.*

De var med sitt barn. *They were with their (own) child.*

but: De var med deras barn. *They were with their (someone else's) child.*

Using it incorrectly can sometimes be embarrassing as the second examples might suggest.

The word *sig* is used with reflexive phrases:

Hon befann sig brevid honom. *She found herself next to him.*

ÖVNINGAR

I.   Fyll i de rätta prepositionerna (Fill in the correct prepositions).

  1. Boken jag läste var _____ Rydberg.
  2. Jag är _____ USA nu.
  3. Vi äter efterrätt _____ middagen.
  4. Är du _____ Kalifornien?
  5. De pratar _____ dig.
  6. Du har inte pratat _____ mig på hela dagen.
  7. Kan du inte köpa en bok _____ mig?
  8. Jag kan träffa dig _____ tågstationen.

II. Fyll i de rätta tidssatserna (Fill in the correct time phrases).

  1. (for) Jag har läst svenska _____ en månad nu.
  2. (in) Han sa att han ska åka till Sverige _____ en vecka.
  3. (last spring) Jag var där _____.
  4. (yesterday) Han talade med mig _____.
  5. (this spring) Min mor åker till Sverige _____.
  6. (tomorrow) Eva träffar Erik _____.
  7. (last Wednesday) Jag var ute med Eva _____.

III. Fyll i de rätta orden *sin - sitt - sina* (Fill in the right words).

  1. (own) Han har _____ vykort.
  2. (someone else's) Hon har_____ tröja.
  3. (own) Hon talar med _____ mamma.
  4. (someone else's) De äter _____ middag.
  5. (own) De pratar med _____ barn.
  6. (someone else's) De köpte _____ hus.

IV. Fyll i rätta orden *sin - hans - hennes* (Fill in the right words. Make sure
     that the subject is the same person!).

1. Stefan sa till Eva att han skulle titta efter _____ barn. (Evas)
2. Erik ska åka med _____ fru Anna till USA. (Eriks)
3. Erik och _____ fru åker nästa vecka. (Eriks)
4. Pepe talade med en kvinna som tycker att _____ hus är stor.
   (kvinnans)
5. Mikael har sagt till Lisa att han ska hämta _____ post när hon
   är i Sverige med _____ barn. (Lisas, Lisas)

V.   Fyll i rätta orden *gång - tid* (Fill in the right words).

1. Hur många _____ har du varit till Sverige?
2. Hur lång _____ tar det att komma dit?
3. Tar det mycket _____ att göra dina övningar?
4. Jag har ätit två _____ idag.
5. Jag har sett filmen fem _____.

VI. Översätt till svenska (Translate into Swedish).

1. Sorry I am late.
2. Pleased to meet you.
3. Where can I buy some postcards?
4. Do you have any stamps?
5. I would like to introduce you to Mr. Berg.

VII. Översätt till engelska (Translate into English).

1. Skulle damen vilja ha ett glas vin?
2. Skulle du vilja fika?
3. Du kan skicka en e-post härifrån.
4. Vi har inga telefonkort.
5. Det är slut på frimärken.

ETYMOLOGY

In Sweden it is common in formal situations to use the third person when addressing someone. Do not be surprised if you are the only woman in the room and you hear someone ask *Would the lady like some coffee?—Skulle damen vilja ha kaffe?* Or, as the only male, you hear *Would the man like to have tea?—Skulle herrn vilja ha te?* They are addressing you.

As things change in a culture, so do words. Sometimes words refer to things the way they were at a previous time. The word for breakfast in Swedish is a borrowed word from German from when many Germans lived in Sweden in thirteenth and fourteenth centuries. Literally *frukost* means early meal. The word commonly used for dinner, *middag*, used to be the large meal eaten in the middle of the day, hence the meaning of the word literally midday. As the society changed from agrarian to industrial, however, the word for the big meal one ate stayed the same though the time did not. Further, a new word was needed to take the place of the old word for the now smaller meal eaten in the middle of the day. The Swedes borrowed a word from another language, namely English, hence the word *lunch*.

Holidays

The calendar is filled with holidays throughout the year. Since Sweden is a dark place in the winter, many holidays celebrate the sun in summer or long for its return in winter. Most have religious significance.

The first holiday season of the year includes Lent and Easter. During Lent Swedes eat a roll, called a *semla*. *Semlor* began as a treat to be eaten before the Lenten fast, but now are eaten only during Lent. They are a lightly sweetened roll with cream in the middle. They are good, but be careful not to eat too many. Legend has it, one king of Sweden ate so many that his stomach burst.

After Lent is Easter. During Easter, children dress up as the Easter witch, *påskkäring*, and go from house to house to get candy, rather like Halloween in the United States. It is also one of the two days that many Swedes actually go to church.

After Easter comes *Valborgsmässoafton*, Walpurgis night, on the 30th of April. People gather to light a bonfire and celebrate the coming of spring and the end of the long winter. The following day is May Day. May Day, like Labor Day in the United States, celebrates the successes of the labor movement in making life better for workers.

One of the most typically Swedish holidays is Midsummer. Midsummer is usually on June 20th and is the longest day of the year. On this day in the north the sun does not set. In the south the sun sets only for a few hours. On this day Swedes celebrate the glorious summer by dancing around a "May pole" decorated with flowers and streamers.

In the fall the sun wanes and celebrations often have to do with light and feasting. On *Mårtensafton*, Martin's eve, people gather to eat goose and a blood soup that is spiced to taste like a gingersnap. This tradition is mainly found in Skåne in the South of Sweden. By December the sun comes up for only a few hours. In the North it does not come up at all. The 13th of December is

Luciadagen, celebrating the triumphant return of this obscure Italian saint, Saint Lucia, after her martyrdom. Why is she celebrated in Sweden? Because upon her return she was seen with lights in her hair. On this day students, who have usually been up all night, come to the houses of their teachers with *pepparkakor* (gingersnaps) and coffee early in the morning to sing the song *Sankta Lucia*.

Christmas is a big holiday in Sweden, again celebrated with light. Whereas *Luciadagen* is a holiday for friends, Christmas is a holiday for family. Traditionally on Christmas eve families dance around the tree singing *nu är det jul igen*, now it is Christmas again. In the good old days, they opened their presents and early Christmas morning took a sleigh ride to church.

The year ends and begins with New Year's Eve and New Year's Day. On this day many Swedes watch fireworks and dance in the new year with a waltz.

LESSON
8

SAMTAL I

Affärer.

Före mötet:

FRU LINDQUIST: Är pappren till mötet klara?

HERR ANDERSSON: Ja, jag är nästan klar. Jag har gjort kopior åt alla och jag
                  har satt upp datorn där inne till presentationen.

FRU LINDQUIST: Har du kontrollerat videoapparaten?

HERR ANDERSSON: Nej, men jag kan göra det nu.

FRU LINDQUIST: Jag tycker att det vore bra. Det blir ingen bra presentation
                  om inte videoapparaten fungerar.

HERR ANDERSSON: Är du nervös?

FRU LINDQUIST: Ja, det är jag kanske.

HERR ANDERSSON: Du behöver inte vara det, det blir bra.

FRU LINDQUIST: Nå, Herr Claesson ska vara med.

HERR ANDERSSON: Han sa att han skulle bli försenad. Han hoppas att han
                  kommer vid tretiden.

FRU LINQUIST: Vid tretiden! Då är mötet slut.

HERR ANDERSSON: Han fick inte veta om mötet förrän idag. Han har ett
                  annat möte. Här är pärmarna med alla pappren.

FRU LINDQUIST: Tack.

DIALOGUE I

Business.

Before the meeting:

Ms. LINDQUIST: Are the papers for the meeting ready?

MR. ANDERSSON: Yes, I am almost finished. I have made photocopies for everyone and I have set up the computer inside for the presentation.

Ms. LINDQUIST: Have you checked the VCR?

MR. ANDERSSON: No, but I can do that now.

Ms. LINDQUIST: I think we should. It won't be a very good presentation if the VCR does not work.

MR. ANDERSSON: Are you nervous?

Ms. LINDQUIST: Yes, perhaps I am.

MR. ANDERSSON: You do not need to be, it will go fine.

Ms. LINDQUIST: Well, Mr. Claesson will be there.

MR. ANDERSSON: He said that he will be late. He hopes he will get here around three o'clock.

Ms. LINQUIST: Three o'clock! By then the meeting will be over.

MR. ANDERSSON: He did not find out about the meeting until today. He has another meeting. Here are the folders with all the files.

Ms. LINDQUIST: Thank you.

SAMTAL II

På mötet:

FRU LINDQUIST: Så som ni kan se, så ökar amerikanska marknaden på mobiltelefoner. Så jag tycker att vi ska kunna öka våra importer till USA.

HERR CLAESSON: Det är mycket bra. Det är ett nöje att göra affärer med USA och jag tycker att det är en marknad som kommer att fortsätta öka i framtiden. Vad precis letar amerikaner efter i en mobiltelefon?

FRU LINDQUIST: Jag tror att det viktigaste är batteriets livstid. Och telefonens räckvidd, men vi har mindre kontroll över det.

HERR CLAESSON: Vi tycker att våra telefoner har bra batterier som håller länge.

FRU LINDQUIST: Så den enda saken är att hålla kostnaden nere. Det är underligt att telefonens kostnad kan vara så låg som den är när man tänker på arbetskostnaderna. Fem veckors semester och allmän sjukförsäkring ökar arbetskostnaderna mycket.

HERR CLAESSON: Jo, men det ökar arbetarnas produktivitet. Nu behöver vi diskutera priser. Här är en prislista över de nya telefoner som vi ska erbjuda.

Fru Lindquist ser över listan:

FRU LINDQUIST: Det blir bra. Så kontraktvillkoren ska vara som jag sa i presentationen.

HERR CLAESSON: Ja, det är godtagbart. Jag ska skicka kontraktet till ditt hotell imorgon.

DIALOGUE II

At the meeting:

MS. LINDQUIST: So as you can see, the American market for cell phones is increasing. So I think that we should be able to increase our imports to the US.

MR. CLAESSON: That's very good. It is a pleasure to do business in the US and I think that it is a market that will continue to grow in the future. What exactly are Americans looking for in a cell phone?

MS. LINDQUIST: I think that the most important thing is the life of the battery. And its range, but we have less control over that.

MR. CLAESSON: We find that our telephones have good batteries that last a long time.

MS. LINDQUIST: So the only thing then is to keep the cost down. It is amazing that the cost of the phone can be as low as it is when one thinks of the labor costs. Five weeks' vacation and national medical increases the labor cost a lot.

MR. CLAESSON: Yes, but it increases the productivity of the workers. Now we need to discuss prices. Here is a price list for the new phones that we will offer.

Ms. Lindquist looks over the list:

MS. LINDQUIST: This looks fine. So the terms of the contract will be as I said in the presentation.

MR. CLAESSON: Yes, that is acceptable. I will send the contract to your hotel tomorrow.

FRU LINDQUIST: Tack för din tid. Det har varit trevligt att göra affärer med dig. Din personal har varit mycket hjälpsam under min vistelse i Stockholm.

HERR CLAESSON: Trevligt att höra.

MS. LINDQUIST: Thank you for your time. It has been a pleasure doing business with you. Your staff has been most helpful during my time in Stockholm.

MR. CLASESSON: I'm glad to hear that.

VOCABULARY

allmän *adj.*	ahllmehn	general/common
amerikan 3 *n. com.*	ahmehrikaanahreh	American
amerikanska *adj.*	ahmehrikaanskah	American
annan *adj.*	ahnahn	another
arbetare (*pl.* -are) *n. com.*	ahrbehtahreh	worker
arbetskostnad 3 *n. com.*	ahrbehtskohstnahd	labor costs
batteri 3 *n. neu.*	bahttehree	battery
behöva IIa *v.*	behhurvah	need
dess *pro.*	dehss	its
diskutera I *v.*	diskutayrah	discuss
enda *adj.*	ehndah	only
erbjuda IV u-ö-u *v.*	ayrbyewdah	offer
fortsätta IV ä-a-ä *v.*	fohrtsehttah	continue
framtid 3 *n. com.*	frahmteed	future
fungera I *v.*	fungehrah	work/function
förrän *conj.*	ferrrehn	until
godtagbar *adj.*	goodtaagbahr	acceptable
hjälpsam *adj.*	yehlpsahm	helpful
hoppas I *v.*	hohppahs	hope
höra IIa *v.*	hurrah	hear
import 3 *n. com.*	impohrt	import
ingen *adj.*	ingehn	no
klar *adj.*	klaar	ready/finished/clear
kontrakt 5 *n. neu.*	kohntrahkt	contract
kontraktvillkor 5 *n. neu.*	kohntrahktvillkoar	contract conditions
kontroll 3 *n. com.*	kohntrohll	control
kontrollera I *v.*	kohntrohlehrah	check
kopia 1 *n. com.*	kohpeeah	copy
kostnad 3 *n. com.*	kohstnahd	cost
leta I *v.*	laytah	search
lista 1 *n. com.*	listah	list
livstid 3 *n. com.*	livsteed	lifetime
låg *adj.*	loag	low

marknad 3 *n. com.*	**mah**rknahd	market
medicin 3 *n. com.*	mehdis**een**	medicine
mobiltelefon 3 *n. com.*	mohb**ee**ltehlehfoan	cell phone
möte 4 *n. neu.*	**mur**teh	meeting
nervös *adj.*	nehr**vur**s	nervous
nöje 4 *n. neu.*	**nur**yeh	pleasure
om *prep.*	ohm	about
papper 5 *n.neu.*	**pah**ppehr	paper
precis *adv.*	prehs**ees**	exactly
presentation 3 *n. com.*	prehsehntahsh**oon**	presentation
pris 3 *n. com.*	prees	price
produktivitet 5 *n. neu.*	prohduktivit**ayt**	productivity
pärm 2 *n. com.*	**pehrm**	folder
redo (undeclineable) *adj.*	**ray**doh	ready
räckvidd *n. com.*	**reh**kkvidd	range
sjukförsäkring 2 *n. com.*	shewkferrrsh**eh**kring	health insurance
slut 5 *n. com.*	slewt	finish/end
sätta upp IV	**seh**ttaa upp	set up
(sätter-satte-satt) *v.*		
tid 3 *n. com.*	teed	time
underlig *adj.*	**u**ndehrlig	strange
USA	ewehsaa	USA
semester 2 *n. com.*	sehm**eh**stehr	vacation
videoapparat 3 *n. com.*	**vee**dehohahppahr**aat**	video machine
vistelse 3 *n. com.*	**vi**stehlseh	stay
vore (from vara) *v.*	**voo**reh	were
öka I *v.*	**er**kah	increase

USEFUL EXPRESSIONS

Jag är född i ...	I was born in ...
Jag låg vid ... universitet.	I went to the university of ...
Mitt huvudämne var ...	My major was ...
biologi	biology
handel	business
kemi	chemistry
datorkunskap	computer science
geografi	geography
internationella relationer	international relations
litteratur	literature
matematik	mathematics
fysik	physics
vetenskap	science
Jag söker jobb.	I am looking for a job.

GRAMMAR

1. Comparison of Adverbs

Like adjectives, some adverbs can also be used in comparative statements and they are also formed in much the same way. Below are a few examples of comparative adverbs:

högt *highly*	högre	högst
konstigt *strangely*	konstigare	konstigast
trevligt *pleasantly*	trevligare	trevligast

Note that in English we usually form the comparisons *more pleasantly* and *most pleasantly.*

Some adverbs not formed from adjectives can also be made into the comparison forms:

fort *quickly*	fortare	fortast
ofta *often*	oftare	oftast

A few adverbs, like the adjectives, have special forms for the comparison:

bra *well*	bättre	bäst
gärna *gladly*	hellre	helst
illa *badly*	värre	värst
mycket *very*	mer(a)	mest
nära *near*	närmare	närmast

1.1   MORE ON ADVERBS

A final word on adverbs. There are a few adverbs that should be discussed briefly. The English word *then* is translated into Swedish with two words: *då,* which means *at that time*, and *sedan*, which means *after that*:

> Jag ringde klockan två. Du var inte hemma då.
> *I called at two o'clock. You were not home then.*

but Vi var hemma. Sedan gick vi till affären.
> *We were at home. Then we went to the store.*

In English we use the word *when* both as an interrogative and as a subordinate conjuction. Swedish uses *var* for the interrogative and *där* for the conjunction:

> Var bor du?
> *Where do you live?*

But: Det finns en restaurang där vi kan äta.
> *There is a restaurant where we can eat.*

2.   Conjunctions

Conjunctions in Swedish, like English, can be divided into two groups: coordinating conjunctions, which introduce independent clauses, and subordinating conjuctions, which introduce dependent clauses.

The coordinating conjunctions in Swedish are:

eller *or*	för *for*	men *but*	och *and*
så *so*	ty *for*	utan *but/except*	

Note that *ty* is rather archaic and seldom used.

The subordinating conjunctions are:

att *that*	då *when*
då *as/since*	därför att *because*
eftersom *as/since*	fast *or* fastän *although*
för att *in order that*	förrän *until*
innan *before*	medan *while*
när *when*	om *if*
sedan *after*	så att *so that*
tills *until*	trots att *in spite of the fact that*

It is important to know if a conjunction is coordinating or subordinating as this will have an effect on the word order. This will be dealt with in Lesson 10.

ÖVNINGAR

I.   Fyll i de rätta adverben *var* eller *där* (Fill in the correct adverb).

   1. _____ ska du vara idag?
   2. Jag vill vara _____ jag kan bli glad.
   3. _____ ligger affären?
   4. Affären ligger _____.
   5. Jag vill vara _____ jag kan äta.

II. Fyll i den rätta bisatskonjunktionen (Fill in the correct subordinating conjunction).

   1. (because) Jag gick till restaurangen _____ jag var hungrig.
   2. (since) Jag gick hem _____ min mor sa att jag måste.
   3. (until) Du var ute _____ du gick hem.
   4. (in order to) Du kom hem _____ ringa mig.
   5. (although) Din mor sa att du måste vara hemma _____ du ville vara ute.

III. Fyll i den rätta huvudsatskonjunktionen (Fill in the correct coordinating conjunction).

   1. (or) Vill du äta _____ sova.
   2. (for) Du kom hem _____ du är bra.
   3. (but) Jag ville äta middag ute _____ du ville äta inne.
   4. (and) Jag var hemma _____ du var ute.

IV. Skriv adverb som komparativ (Write the adverb as a comparative).

   1. (most pleasantly) Han skrev _____ av oss alla.
   2. (best) Hon läser _____.
   3. (more often) Jag vill resa _____.
   4. (nearer) Jag vill bo _____ dig.
   5. (more) Du äter _____!

V.   Översätt till svenska (Translate into Swedish).

1. Are you ready for the meeting?
2. Have you checked the computer?
3. Are you nervous?
4. You should check the battery.
5. Do you have a cell phone?

VI.   Översätt till engelska (Translate into English).

1. Jag har gjort kopiorna.
2. Vi har ingen dator.
3. Jag ska inte vara där idag.
4. Man får fem veckors semester i Sverige.
5. Du har varit mycket hjälpsam.

ETYMOLOGY

All languages need to create new words for new concepts. How each language accomplishes the creation of new words can sometimes be interesting. All languages have needed to keep up with vocabulary for new innovations that have been made in computers and technology. Icelandic, another Scandinavian language, has very successfully created new vocabulary from native root words. The word for computer in Icelandic is *tölva*, a combination of the words *telja* meaning to count and *völva* meaning to foresee or prophecy. Swedish has most often simply borrowed words from the language from which the concept comes. Words like *internetkafé* and *surfa på internet* (sometimes spelled *internät*) hardly need translating for the English speaker since they are so close to the English equivalents. In some cases the words or phrases start out as a borrowing and then, through time, become Swedish. Years ago in Sweden one spoke of *e-mail* and now it has become *e-post* using the more common Swedish word for mail, *post*. In some cases, however, the Swedish academy has attempted to construct words using Swedish roots, much in the same way as Icelandic. The word for computer, *dator*, was one such attempt. The Swedish Academy tried in the late seventies to create a productive class of words ending in *-or*. Words like *dator* were to represent a class of words for mechanical things, similar to the latin ending in *motor*. This attempt to construct language was only a minor success.

Education and Research

Education is highly funded and highly respected in Sweden. In 1997, Sweden spent 37.6 billion kronor, or 4.7 billion dollars, on higher education. The fundamental principle in Swedish education is that all children and young people should have equal access to it regardless of where in the country they live. Schooling starts at age seven and is mandatory until the age of 16. Secondary school starts after nine years of compulsory school and can be divided into three main university tracks: natural sciences, social sciences, and technology. There are also a number of vocational tracks, including business and administration, construction, child recreation, electrical engineering, health care, media programming, and natural resource use programs to name a few.

After secondary school, the young person can go to university, if he or she was in a university track, or a vocational college of which there are many in Sweden. It is always possible to take courses as an adult to retrain or continue training and this is done a lot in Sweden. Tuition for all higher education in Sweden is at little or no cost to the student, though student loans are often taken for housing, food, and incidentals.

There are a number of world-class universities in Sweden, including Stockholm University, Gothenburg University, Lund, Uppsala, Umeå, and others. Students at university pay only a minimal student union fee, usually around 200 dollars a year. These universities have a large student body and also have many students from other countries who have come there to study. The total number of undergraduates matriculated at universities throughout Sweden in 1997 was 300,400, of which 37% were studying law and social sciences, 20% were studying humanities and theology, 17% natural sciences, 13% technology, 7% paramedical, 3% medicine, and 2% artistic and practical/aesthetic education.

Two areas in which Swedish education and research excel are technology and medicine. One of the best sites for education in the world for medicine is the Karolinska Institute in Stockholm. For technology a world leader is Chalmers in Gothenburg.

LESSON
9

SAMTAL I

Några ärende.

Fru Lindquist vill tacka Monika Andersson för hjälpen hon har gett de senaste fem dagarna genom att laga middag åt henne:

FRU ANDERSSON: Donna, vad behöver vi till din middag ikväll?

FRU LINDQUIST: Pasta, salt, olja, vinäger, socker, mjölk, smör, bröd och köttfärs.

FRU ANDERSSON: Okej, men jag behöver några saker också.

FRU LINDQUIST: Fint, som vad då?

FRU ANDERSSON: (*Tittar på listan*) Jag behöver senap, ketchup, honung, ägg, tandkräm, servetter, toalettpapper och tvättmedel.

FRU LINDQUIST: Lägg dem i min korg bara. Du har varit så vänlig mot mig denna vecka.

FRU ANDERSSON: Säkert?

FRU LINDQUIST: Ja.

FRU ANDERSSON: Bra, men då köper jag vinet. Är det något speciellt vin du föredrar?

FRU LINDQUIST: Ett franskt vin vore bra.

FRU ANDERSSON: Då behöver vi gå till Systembolaget. Man kan köpa endast öl på affärer.

FRU LINDQUIST: Bra, jag följer med dig.

FRU ANDERSSON: Fint.

DIALOGUE I

A few errands.

Ms. Lindquist wants to thank Monika Andersson for all the help she has given for the past five days by making dinner for her:

Ms. Andersson: Donna, what do we need for your dinner tonight?

Ms. Lindquist: Pasta, salt, oil, vinegar, sugar, milk, butter, bread and hamburger.

Ms. Andersson: Ok, and I need a few things too.

Ms. Lindquist: Fine, like what?

Ms. Andersson: (*Looks at her list*) I need mustard, ketchup, honey, eggs, toothpaste, napkins, toilet paper, and laundry soap.

Ms. Lindquist: Just put them in my cart. You have been so nice to me this past week.

Ms. Andersson: Are you sure?

Ms. Lindquist: Yes.

Ms. Andersson: Ok, but I will buy the wine. Is there a special kind you would like?

Ms. Lindquist: A French wine would be nice.

Ms. Andersson: We will have to go to the state liquor store then. You can only buy beer in the grocery stores.

Ms. Lindquist: Ok, I'll follow you.

Ms. Andersson: Ok.

SAMTAL II

Vinces hår har blivit för långt och han vill klippa sig så han och Eva går till frisören:

FRISÖREN: Vad kan jag stå till tjänst med?

VINCE: Ja, jag skulle vilja klippa mig.

EVA: Varför gör du inte någonting vilt som att färga håret eller permanenta dig?

VINCE: Nej, det tänker jag inte göra.

EVA: Varför inte, det vore kul. (*Till frisören*) Hur mycket kostar det att permanenta sig?

FRISÖREN: Sex hundra kronor.

VINCE: Det var mycket, jag tror att jag ska klippa mig bara.

EVA: (*Eva struntar i Vince och pratar med frisören*) Att färga håret, hur mycket kostar det?

FRISÖREN: Tre hundra.

VINCE: Vad kostar en vanlig klippning?

FRISÖREN: Två hundra.

EVA: Jag betalar för att färga ditt hår, vi färgar det blont.

FRISÖREN: Jag rekommenderar denna färg.

EVA: Har du någonting ljusare?

DIALOGUE II

Vince's hair is getting a little long and he wants to have it cut, so he and Eva go to the barber's:

BARBER: May I help you?

VINCE: Yes, I'd like to have my hair cut.

EVA: Why don't you do something wild like having it dyed or having a perm?

VINCE: No, I don't think so.

EVA: Why not, it could be fun. (*To the barber*) How much does it cost to have a perm?

BARBER: Six hundred crowns.

VINCE: That's a lot. I think I will only have it cut.

EVA: (*Eva ignores Vince and talks to the barber*) What about dyed, how much is that?

BARBER: Three hundred.

VINCE: How much for a regular haircut?

BARBER: Two hundred.

EVA: I'll pay to have your hair dyed; let's dye it blond.

BARBER: I suggest this color.

EVA: Do you have anything lighter?

FRISÖREN: Visst, hur vore det med den här?

EVA: Den där färgen är fin.

FRISÖREN: (*Till Vince*) Skulle du också vilja ha manikyr?

VINCE: Jag vill bara klippa mig!

EVA: Vad tråkigt.

Barber: Yes, what about this?

Eva: That color is nice.

Barber: (*To Vince*) Would you also like a manicure?

Vince: I only want my hair cut!

Eva: How boring.

VOCABULARY

blond *adj.*	blohnd	blond
bröd 5 *n. neu.*	brerrd	bread
fransk *adj.*	frahnsk	French
frisör 3 *n. com.*	freese**rr**	barber
färg 2 *n. com.*	fehry	color
färga I *v.*	**feh**rya	color
föredra (~drar-~drog- ~dragit) *v.*	**fe**rrehdrah	prefer
honung 2 *n. com.*	**hoh**nung	honey
hår 5 *n. neu.*	hoar	hair
ketchup 3 *n. com.*	**keh**chup	ketchup
klippa sig *v.*	**klip**pah say	have one's hair cut
klippning 2 *n. com.*	**klip**pning	haircut
korg 2 *n. com.*	**koh**ry	cart
köttfärs 3 *n. com.*	she**rt**tfehrsh	hamburger
laga I *v.*	**laa**gah	fix
ljus *adj.*	yews	light
manikyr 3 *n. com.*	mahni**ki**r	manicure
mjölk 2 *n. com.*	**my**erlk	milk
olja 1 *n. com.*	**oh**lyah	oil
pasta 1 *n. com.*	**pah**stah	pasta
permanenta sig I *v.*	pehrmahn**eh**ntah say	have a perm
salt (*pl.* salter) *n. neu.*	sahlt	salt
senap 3 *n. com.*	**seh**nahp	mustard
senaste *adj.*	**say**nahsteh	latest
servett 3 *n. com.*	sehrv**eh**tt	napkins
slags 5 *n. neu.*	slahks	sort
smör 5 *n. neu.*	smerr	butter
socker 5 *n. neu.*	**soh**kkehr	sugar
strunta I *v.*	**strun**tah	ignore
Systembolaget	sist**ay**mbool**aa**geht	state liquor store
säkert *adv.*	**say**kehrt	certainly
tacka I *v.*	**tah**kkah	thank
tandkräm *n. com.*	**tah**ndkraym	toothpaste

tjänst 3 *n. com.*	shehnst	service
toalettpapper 5 *n. neu.*	tohahl**eh**tpahppehr	toilet paper
tråkig *adj.*	tr**oa**kig	boring
tvättmedel 5 *n. neu.*	tv**eh**ttmaydehl	laundry soap
vanlig *adj.*	v**aa**nlig	ordinary
vild *adj.*	vild	wild
vinäger 2 *n. com.*	vin**ay**gehr	vinegar
vänlig *adj.*	v**eh**nlig	friendly/nice
ägg 5 *n. neu.*	ehgg	egg
öl 5 *n. neu.*	erl	beer

USEFUL EXPRESSIONS

Jag vill köpa ...	I would like to buy ...
Jag försöker hitta ...	I am trying to find ...
huvudvärkstabletter	aspirin
plåster	Band-Aids
halspastiller	cough drops
eye liner	eye liner
ögonpenna	eye pencil
ögonskugga	eye shadow
fotkräm	foot cream
läppstift	lipstick
smink	make-up
munvatten	mouthwash
nagelklippare	nail clipper
nagelfil	nail file
tidning	newspaper
rakhyvel	razor
säkerhetsnålar	safety pins
rakborste	shaving brush
rakkräm	shaving cream
raktvål	shaving soap
tvål	soap
solkräm	suntan lotion
termometer	thermometer
pappersnäsdukar	tissues
tandborste	toothbrush
handduk	towel
pincett	tweezers
ost	cheese
kött	meat
frukt	fruit
äpple	apple
banan	banana
apelsin	orange
jos	juice

GRAMMAR

1. Reflexive Phrases

Some verbs in Swedish are found with reflexive pronouns, which means that the subject and the object are the same:

Jag har klippt mig.	*I have had my hair cut.*
Jag har klippt dig.	*I cut your hair.*
Jag gifter mig med dig.	*I am marrying you.*
Jag gifter dig.	*I am marrying you (i.e. I am the minister).*
Jag lär mig svenska	*I am learning Swedish.*
Jag lär dig svenska	*I am teaching you Swedish.*

Below are a list of common verbs used with reflexive pronouns in Swedish:

beklaga sig *complain*
föreställa sig *imagine*
gifta sig *marry*
känna sig *feel*
lära sig *learn*
raka sig *shave*
skynda sig *hurry*
ta av sig *take off*
tänka sig *imagine*
vända sig *turn*

bry sig *care about*
förlova sig *get engaged*
klippa sig *cut hair*
lägga sig *lie down*
permanenta sig *get a perm*
röra sig *move*
sätta sig *sit down*
ta på sig *put on*
visa sig *appear*
öva sig *practice*

2. S-Verbs

There are three different possible uses for the s-form of verbs. One use has been described above and is a passive voice:

Boken läses av mig.	*The book was read by me.*
Brevet skrevs av dig.	*The letter was written by you.*

Another use is with reciprocal meaning, this means that the verbs can be used to express a reciprocal action:

Vi träffas imorgon.	*We will see each other tomorrow.*
Vi ses.	*We will see each other* or *I'll see you.*
Vi hörs.	*We will hear each other* or *I'll talk to you (later).*

Finally there are some verbs called deponent verbs. They have a passive form but are active in meaning. The deponant verbs in Swedish are:

hoppas *to hope*	lyckas *to succeed*
låtsas *to pretend*	minnas *to remember*
synas *to seem*	trivas *to thrive*
tyckas *to seem*	

EXAMPLES:

Jag hoppas att hon kommer.	*I hope that she comes.*
Han lyckades köpa mat.	*He succeeded in buying food.*
Jag minns inte var bilen är.	*I do not remember where the car is.*

3. The Verb *lära*

The verb *lära* when used as an auxiliary verb has the meaning *it is said to*:

Hon lär vara vacker.	*She is said to be beautiful.*
Boken lär vara bra.	*The book is said to be good.*

4. Participles

Like English, Swedish has past and present participles. Participles are used like adjectives.

Present participles are simply made by adding *-ande* to the end of the root stem of conjugations I, II, and IV, and *-ende* to conjugation III (remember that conjugation III stems end in a vowel):

I talande	en talande man *a talking man*
II ringande	en ringande klocka *a ringing clock*
III troende	en troende man *a believing man*
IV skrivande	en skrivande kvinna *a writing woman*

Remember that Swedish does not have a construction equivalent to *is going*, and therefore a sentence like *han är gående* should be translated *he is a walking person.*

Past participles are declined for gender and number and are formed in the following way:

	COMMON	NEUTER	PLURAL/DEFINITE
I	talad	talat	talade
IIa	ringd	ringt	ringda
IIb	köpt	köpt	köpta
III	trodd	trott	trodda
IV	skriven	skrivet	skrivna

EXAMPLES:
en omdiskuterad kvinna *a much discussed woman*
ett köpt hus *a bought house*
ett trott barn *a believed child*
två skrivna böcker *two written books.*

ÖVNINGAR

I. Skriv de följande reflexiva verben i rätt form (Write the following reflexive verbs in the right form).

1. (lära sig) Han har _____ bra svenska.
2. (klippa sig) Jag vill _____ för att mitt hår är för långt.
3. (raka sig) _____!
4. (känna sig) Hur _____ du _____?
5. (skynda sig) Han måste _____. Vi är försenade.

II. Fyll i rätta formen, s-verb eller inte (Use the right form, s-verb or not).

1. (träffa) Jag ska _____ honom imorgon.
2. (träffa) Vi _____ hemma.
3. (se) Vi _____ sedan.
4. (se) Hon _____ honom under bordet.
5. (tycka) Han _____ att han är bra.
6. (tycka) Han _____ vara bra.

III. Skriv presens particip till följande verb (Write the present participle for the following verbs).

1. skriva _____
2. köpa _____
3. prata _____
4. tro _____
5. bo _____
6. äta_____

IV. Skriv perfekt particip till följande verb (Write the past participle for the following verbs, write all the forms).

1. dricka _____
2. fråga _____
3. förlåta _____

4. hjälpa _____
5. komma _____
6. tro_____

V. Översätt till svenska (Translate into Swedish).

1. I would like a haircut.
2. What do we need for dinner?
3. How much is a perm?
4. What sort of wine would you like for dinner?
5. Could I get a manicure?

VI. Översätt till engelska (Translate into English).

1. Du kan köpa vin på Systembolaget.
2. Vi har ingen pasta i den här affären.
3. Vilken färg vill du färga håret med?
4. Du skulle se bra ut som blond.
5. Jag kan inte rekommendera det.

ETYMOLOGY

English derives participles in much the same way as in Swedish. A thousand years ago there were two differing dialects of Old English, one that formed its present participles -*and* and another -*ing*. Obviously the -*ing* form is the only ending to survive in Modern English. In Swedish the ending is -*and*.

In English, past participles are formed in much the same way as Swedish. Strong verbs like *write* and *freeze* are formed from the perfect tense of the verb to yield phrases like: *a written book* and *a frozen pie*, from the perfect tense *has written* and *has frozen*. In Swedish these same phrases are *en skriven bok* and *en frusen paj*, from the perfect forms *har skrivit* and *har frusit*. They are similar except for the fact that Swedish declines its adjectives. Weak verbs are formed with -*d*, Swedish *en plockad kyckling*, which should be reminiscent of English -*ed*, *a plucked chicken*.

Like English speakers, Swedish speakers do not always speak prescriptively (what some might call wrong). In certain dialects you might more frequently hear someone say *Jag ska tala vid han* (I am going to talk to him) instead of the more prescriptive *Jag ska tala med honom*. Another example is the gender of the word *öl* (beer). Though the Swedish Academy says that the gender is *ett*, you will hear more people asking for *en öl* than those asking for *ett öl*. The reason is that you usually ask for a can *en burk* or a bottle *en flaska* of beer. Since these words are *en* words, by extension the word *öl* itself has become associated with *en* instead of *ett*.

Everyday Life

Everyday life in Sweden is not altogether different from life in the United States. There are, however, some things that make most Americans pause when they first encounter them.

Swedes are not inclined to eat sweet things for breakfast, like muffins and Danish pastries (ironically, Danish pastries in Sweden are called Viennese bread, Swedish *wienerbröd*). These sweeter things are usually eaten with coffee in the middle of the day. It would not be uncommon for a Swede to eat toast with cheese, rather than jam, and pickled herring for breakfast. For a lighter breakfast try muesli, not unlike granola.

It can be expensive to go out to a restaurant for dinner, so Swedes usually do this less frequently than in the U.S. It is not as expensive to go out to lunch, therefore many more Swedes eat lunch out. Unlike the United States where ordering out is like a game of 20 Questions, there are often fewer choices at restaurants, called *dagens rätt* or the meal of the day. Since lunch often ends up being rather large, it is not uncommon for dinner to be light fare.

Swedes drink a lot of coffee, and strong coffee. Many Americans when traveling in Sweden are surprised at the strength of Swedish coffee given the weakness of the coffee served by their Midwestern descendants. It has been suggested that though coffee was important to the immigrants that came to this country in the nineteenth century, perhaps because it reminded them of home, it was difficult to come by and often expensive. One way to make it last longer was to make weaker coffee. In Sweden coffee is often drunk with a sweet to go with it. It is a social occasion as well, so much so that the Swedes have a special word for going out with friends and having coffee and sweets, *fika.*

Swedes like to read newspapers. Many Swedes subscribe to and read two newspapers a day. The newspapers in Sweden are attached to the political parties, so you always know from what viewpoint the newspaper is looking at an issue. The two major newpapers are *Dagens Nyheter*, affiliated with the Social Democratic Party, and *Svenska Dagbladet*, published by the Moderates. *Expressen* and *Aftonbladet* are two newspapers not attached to a political party, but they also are considered more popular newspapers, and not as serious as the others. It is not uncommon to find Swedes during their coffee breaks reading these papers in the break room.

LESSON
10

SAMTAL I

Att resa.

Efter att ha avslutat sina affärer kommer fru Lindquist att resa till Kiruna för att se midnattsolen. Hon hälsar på SAS kontoret och frågar efter flygresor:

FRU LINDQUIST: Jag skulle vilja fråga om flygresor.

EXPEDITEN: Inrikes eller utrikes?

FRU LINDQUIST: Inrikes, jag skulle vilja åka till Kiruna.

EXPEDITEN: När skulle du vilja åka?

FRU LINDQUIST: Imorgon om det finns lediga platser.

EXPEDITEN: Ja visst finns det platser. Skulle du vilja resa första klass eller ekonomi?

FRU LINDQUIST: Hur mycket kostar första klass?

EXPEDITEN: Första klass kostar 5 500 kronor.

FRU LINDQUIST: Då tar jag första klass. Hur dags går flyget?

EXPEDITEN: Imorgon bitti klockan 8:30. När vill du resa tillbaka?

FRU LINDQUIST: Om jag åker imorgon skulle jag vilja komma tillbaka om tre dagar, på söndag.

EXPEDITEN: Fint, det går bra. Här får du dina biljetter.

Vid ankomsten till flygplatsen i Kiruna går Fru Lindquist till bilexpediten för att hyra en bil.

DIALOGUE I

Traveling.

Having finished her business, Ms. Lindquist is going to take a side trip to Kiruna to see the midnight sun. She visits the Scandinavian Airlines office to ask about flights:

Ms. LINDQUIST: I would like to inquire about a flight.

AGENT: Domestic or international?

Ms. LINDQUIST: Domestic. I would like to go to Kiruna.

AGENT: When would you like to go?

Ms. LINDQUIST: Tomorrow if there are any seats available.

AGENT: Oh yes, there are seats. Would you like first class or economy?

Ms. LINDQUIST: How much is first class?

AGENT: First class is 5,500 crowns.

Ms. LINDQUIST: I will take first class then. What time does that flight leave?

AGENT: Tomorrow at 8:30 in the morning. When would you like to return?

Ms. LINDQUIST: If I leave tomorrow, I would like to return in three days, on Sunday.

AGENT: Ok, you are all set, here are your tickets.

Upon arrival in Kiruna airport, Ms. Lindquist goes to the car agent to rent a car.

FRU LINDQUIST: Jag skulle vilja hyra en bil tack.

EXPEDITEN: Vilken sorts bil ville du ha?

FRU LINDQUIST: Har du en SAAB?

EXPEDITEN: Ja visst har vi SAAB. Jag behöver se ditt körkort.

FRU LINDQUIST: Jaha, behöver jag ett internationellt körkort?

EXPEDITEN: Nej, ditt amerikanska körkort går bra. Hur många dagar ville du ha bilen?

FRU LINDQUIST: Bara idag och imorgon.

EXPEDITEN: Okej, det blir 1676,25 kronor om dagen med försäkring.

FRU LINDQUIST: Herre Gud det var mycket!

EXPEDITEN: Det är normalt pris i Sverige.

FRU LINDQUIST: Jag tar den.

EXPEDITEN: Var snäll och skriv under kontraktet.

MS. LINDQUIST: I'd like to rent a car.

AGENT: What type do you prefer?

MS. LINDQUIST: Do you have a SAAB?

AGENT: Oh yes, we have SAABs. I will have to see your license.

MS. LINDQUIST: Oh, do I have to have an international license?

AGENT: No, your American license will be fine. How many days would you like the car?

MS. LINDQUIST: Only today and tomorrow.

AGENT: Ok, that will be 1676.25 crowns a day with the insurance.

MS. LINDQUIST: My God, that's a lot!

AGENT: That is the standard price in Sweden.

MS. LINDQUIST: I'll take it.

AGENT: Sign the contract here please.

SAMTAL II

Vid resans slut bestämmer Vince sig för att åka till Malmö för att få se lite mera av Sverige. Han går till centrala järnvägsstationen i Göteborg för att köpa en biljett:

VINCE: När går nästa tåg till Malmö?

EXPEDIT: Klockan 11:00 på förmiddagen.

VINCE: Jag skulle vilja köpa en biljett tack.

EXPEDIT: Enkel eller tur och retur?

VINCE: Tur och retur.

EXPEDIT: Det är ett intercity tåg. Du behöver en sittplats för detta.

VINCE: Hur mycket kostar det att köpa sittplats?

EXPEDIT: Femtio kronor bara.

VINCE: Och hur mycket kostar biljetten?

EXPEDIT: Femhundra kronor. Om du reser mer denna sommar kan jag rekommendera att du köper ett tågkort. Det kostar etthundra kronor och du får tio procents rabatt. Du sparar femtio kronor på denna resa.

VINCE: Nej tack, jag ska bara resa en enda gång innan jag åker. Så det skulle inte löna sig.

EXPEDIT: Okej. Då blir det femhundrafemtio kronor.

VINCE: Här är sexhundra.

EXPEDIT: Femtio tillbaka och dina biljetter.

VINCE: Tack.

DIALOGUE II

Toward the end of his stay, Vince decides to go to Malmö so that he can see more of Sweden. He goes to the Central Train Station in Gothenburg to buy a ticket:

VINCE: When is the next train to Malmö?

CLERK: At 11:00 this morning.

VINCE: I would like to buy a ticket please.

CLERK: Is that one way or round trip?

VINCE: Round trip.

CLERK: That is an Intercity train. You will need to buy a seat for it.

VINCE: How much does it cost to buy a seat?

CLERK: Only 50 crowns.

VINCE: And how much is the ticket?

CLERK: Five hundred crowns. If you are traveling more this summer, I can recommend that you buy a train card. It costs 100 crowns and you get 10% off. You would save 50 crowns on this trip.

VINCE: No thanks, I am only taking this one trip before I go, so I would not get my money back.

CLERK: Ok. That will be 550 crowns then.

VINCE: Here is 600.

CLERK: Here is 50 and your tickets.

VINCE: Thanks.

VOCABULARY

ankomst 3 *n. com.*	**ah**nkohmst	arrival
avsluta I *v.*	aavslewtah	finish
bestämma sig IIa *v.* (*ref.*)	behst**eh**mmah say	decide
bil 2 *n. com.*	beel	car
bilexpedit 3 *n. com.*	beelehkspehd**ee**t	car agent
biljett 3 *n. com.*	bil**yeh**t	ticket
central *adj.*	sentraal	central
ekonomi 3 *n. com.*	ehkohnohnm**ee**	economy
enda (enda-enda-enda) *adj.*	**eh**ndah	sole/only
enkel *adj.*	**eh**nkehl	single
flyg 5 *n. neu.*	fliwgg	plane
flygresa 1 *n. com.*	fl**iw**ggraysah	plane trip
försäkring 2 *n. com.*	fehrsh**eh**kreeng	insurance
Gud 2 *n. com.*	gewd	God
hyra I *v.*	hirah	rent
hyrespris 5 *n. neu.*	hirehsprees	cost to rent
hälsa på *v.*	h**eh**lsah poa	visit (person)
imorse *adv.*	eem**oh**rshe	this morning
inrikes *adv.*	**in**reekehs	domestic
internationell *adj.*	intehrnahsh**oo**nehll	international
järnvägsstation 3 *n. com.*	**jeh**rnvaygstahshoon	railroad station
klass 3 *n. com.*	klahss	class
körkort 5 *n. neu.*	sh**eh**rrkoort	driver's license
ledig *adj.*	l**ay**deeg	unoccupied
löna sig *v.*	l**eh**rnaa say	to be worthwhile
midnattsol 2 *n. com.*	middnahtts**oo**l	midnight sun
nog *adv.*	noog	probably/I expect to
normal *adj.*	nohrm**aa**l	normal
procent 5 *n. com.*	prohs**eh**nt	percent
rabatt 3 *n. com.*	rahb**ah**tt	rebate
retur *see tur*		
sort 3 *n. com.*	sohrt	sort
snäll *adj.*	snehll	nice

snälla I *v.*	snehllah	be nice
spara I *v.*	sp**aa**rah	save
tur och retur *adv.*	tewr o reht**ewr**	round trip
tåg 5 *n. neu.*	toag	train
tågkort 5 *n. neu.*	t**oa**gkoort	train card
utrikes *adv.*	**ew**treekes	abroad/international

USEFUL EXPRESSIONS

Jag skulle vilja köpa en biljett till Jönköping.	I would like to buy a ticket to Jönköping.
Får studenter rabatt?	Is there a rebate for students?
Får pensionärer rabatt?	Is there a rebate for retired people?
Jag skulle vilja ha en sittplats.	I would like to reserve a seat.
Hur dags ankommer tåget till Kiruna?	What time does the train arrive in Kiruna?
Hur dags landar planet i Arlanda?	What time does the plane land at Arlanda?
Skulle jag kunna få en tidtabell?	Could I have a timetable?
Rökning är förbjuden.	Smoking is forbidden.
Är den här platsen ledig?	Is this seat free?
Jag tror att det här är min plats.	I think this is my seat.
Hur ofta går bussen till Malmö?	How often does the bus go to Malmö?
Var kan jag köpa bensin?	Where can I buy gasoline?

Names of some common European cities

Aten	Athens
Berlin	Berlin
Köpenhamn	Copenhagen
Göteborg	Gothenburg
Helsingfors	Helsinki
London	London
Madrid	Madrid
Moskva	Moscow
München	Munich
Oslo	Oslo
Paris	Paris
Prag	Prague
Rom	Rome
Stockholm	Stockholm

GRAMMAR

1. Sentence Structure

Word order in Swedish is very similar to English; however, it is known as a verb-second language, which means that the verb is always the second part of the sentence. For example:

Jag går hem nu. *I am going home now.*
but Nu går jag hem. *Now I am going home.*

Normal word order in an independent clause is *subject verb object preposition*, however, any of these parts can be placed at the front of the sentence though then the subject must come after the verb:

Jag köpte ett äpple i affären. *I bought an apple in the store.*
Ett äpple köpte jag i affären. *An apple, I bought in the store.*
I affären köpte jag ett äpple. *In the store, I bought an apple.*

Placement of the verb in the initial position makes the sentence a question:

Köpte jag ett äpple i affären? *Did I buy an apple in the store?*

Placement of the adverb is after the verb, though it too can be fronted:

Jag köpte inte ett äpple i affären. *I did not buy an apple in the store.*
Inte köpte jag ett äpple i affären. *I did **not** buy an apple in the store.*

All these sentences have essentially the same meaning but very different emphasis. Further examples:

Jag köpte aldrig äpplen i affären. *I never bought apples in the store.*
Jag köper alltid äpplen i affären. *I always buy apples in the store.*

2. Dependent Clause Word Order

Dependent clauses always have normal word order, that is one can never front parts of a dependent clause. However, placement of adverbs in a dependent clause is before the verb rather than following it:

Jag vet att jag inte köpte ett äpple i affären.
I know that I did not buy an apple in the store.

Jag vet att jag aldrig köper äpplen i affären.
I know that I never buy apples in the store.

ÖVNINGAR

I.   Skriv de följande adverben på rätta platsen (Write the following adverbs in the right place).

   1. (aldrig) Han har varit i Sverige.
   2. (inte) Jag vill köpa en platsbiljett.
   3. (alltid) Jag går till affären.
   4. (sällan) Hon köper pasta.
   5. (ofta) Kommer du hit?

II. Skriv de följande meningarna som bisatser som börjar med "Jag tror att" (Write the following sentences as dependent clauses that begin with "Jag tror att").

   1. Jag ska inte träffa honom imorgon. _____.
   2. Vi äter inte hemma. _____.
   3. Du har inte sett honom. _____.
   4. Hon sitter inte under bordet. _____.
   5. Han är inte bra. _____.
   6. Han har aldrig varit i Sverige. _____.

III. Skriv de följande meningarna så att de börjar med adverbet (Write the following sentences so that they begin with the adverb).

   1. Jag skriver idag.
   2. Jag köpte böckerna igår.
   3. Du måste åka hem nu.
   4. Hon har kommit hem i förrgår.
   5. Han ska åka till Sverige imorgon.
   6. Vi äter nu.

IV. Översätt till svenska (Translate into Swedish).

   1. I would like a ticket to Malmö.
   2. When does the next train go to Stockholm?

3. Do I need a passport to go to Copenhagen?
4. I would like a second class ticket to Gothenburg.
5. Where is the train station?

V.   Översätt till engelska (Translate into English).

1. Tåget går klockan fem.
2. Du får inte hyra en bil här.
3. Du måste ha en biljett.
4. Vilken sorts bil vill du ha?
5. Jag behöver se ditt körkort.

ETYMOLOGY

The verb always is in the second position in Swedish, which may seem odd to the English speaker. However, it was not that long ago that English was also a verb-second language and we have remnants of that even today. Though we do not say "Now go I to the store" in modern English, that is how it was said only a few centuries ago. And English still has constructions like "'I am going now,' said John." Though normal word order would be "John said," it is not strange to an English speaker to end this phrase with "said John."

Swedish has endeavored to call most countries and cities by their local names, thus names like Munich *München* even use letters not found in Swedish. There has even been an attempt in Sweden to change Ireland from the traditional *Irland* to the native word *Eire* with mixed success. There are some exceptions, however. Countries that have been in the Swedish consciousness since ancient times still use their ancient names. One example, the name for France is Swedish is *Frankrike*, literally the kingdom of the Franks. The name for Germany in Swedish is *Tyskland*, actually the same as German *Deutschland* except that the word has undergone a thousand years of sound changes. Also, names ending in *-ia* are often changed to *-ien* in Swedish, thus *Kalifornien*.

Genealogy

In Sweden today, there is hardly anyone who does not have relatives that emigrated and most of them have relatives that emigrated to the United States. Correspondingly, many people in the United States have ancestors that came from Sweden. It has become popular to trace one's lineage back as far as one can. There is help to do this, though there are also some special challenges when one's ancestors came from Scandinavia.

One challenge is the issue of last names in Sweden. Most people in Sweden until relatively recently did not have last names as such, but rather used a patronymic. Therefore if your father's name was Johan and your name was Erik, you would be Erik Johansson. When you had a son and named him Johan, his name would be Johan Eriksson, and so on. To further complicate this problem, many Swedes, when they came to the United States, knowing that there were too many Johan Johanssons, changed their names altogether. Therefore when tracing your family in Sweden, it is important and helpful to know what their name was in Sweden, and also birth dates whenever possible, since you might find several Sven Johanssons in the same parish.

It is also helpful to know where they came from. Until 2000, the church was in charge of birth records in Sweden. In 2000 there was a new mandate that separated church and state. However, for the last two centuries, if one has information on which parish a family member came from, it can be extremely useful in locating records. Another problem is that many of these archives until recently were not centrally located. Many people have gone to Sweden to locate ancestors knowing which parish they come from, only to find that the church has burned down thus ending the search.

There is hope if you are trying to trace your family heritage in Sweden. A few decades ago the emigrant research centers started to pop up in Sweden as Swedes and Americans became interested in finding these long lost connections. One such place is The Kinship Center in Karlstad. To contact them by mail write The Kinship Center, Box 331, S-651 08 Karlstad, Sweden. Or if you are going there, the street address is Hööksgatan 2. Another important research center is The Swedish Emigrant Institute. They have tried to collect as many records as they can and have an excellent collection. To contact them, write to The Swedish Emigrant Institute, PO Box 201, 351 04 Växjö, Sweden. Or call them at Tel: +46 470-201 20, Fax: +46 470-394 16. The Swedish Emigrant Institute has a very enthusiastic and helpful staff.

Some words that may be of importance as you search through family records are:

född *born*	död *dead*
dödsattest *death certificate*	döpt *baptized*
kyrkobokförd *registered in the parish of*	kyrkobokföring *parish registration*
socken *parish*	härad *jurisdictional district*
församling *congregation*	utvandring *emigration*

A few words for family members:

mor *mother*	far *father*
mormor *maternal grandmother*	farmor *paternal grandmother*
morfar *maternal grandfather*	farfar *paternal grandfather*
mormorsmor *maternal great grandmother*	farmorsmor *paternal great grandmother*
syster *sister*	bror *brother*
moster *maternal aunt*	faster *paternal aunt*
morbror *paternal uncle*	farbror *paternal uncle*
son *son*	dotter *daughter*
svåger *brother-in-law*	svägerska *sister-in-law*
syskon *sibling*	kusin *cousin*

KEY TO
EXERCISES

Lesson 1

I.
1. jag
2. dem
3. vi
4. oss
5. hon
6. henne
7. dig
8. ni
9. mig
10. de
11. honom
12. han

II.
1. en
2. ett
3. en
4. en
5. en
6. ett
7. en
8. en
9. en
10. en

III.
1. människor
2. pass
3. chaufförer
4. fruar
5. utbytesstudenter
6. morgnar
7. kompisar
8. problem
9. veckor
10. sidor

IV.
1. väskan
2. dagarna
3. kungarna
4. frun
5. passet
6. hotellet
7. kompisarna
8. året *or* åren
9. veckan
10. kronan

V.
1. Jag talar inte svenska.
2. Han har inte passet.
3. Jag är inte här på semester.
4. Du kan inte få tag på en taxi där.
5. Hon är inte en affärskvinna.

VI.
1. Talar du svenska?
2. Har han passet?
3. Är han här på semester?
4. Kan jag få tag på en taxi där?
5. Är hon en affärskvinna?

Lesson 2

I.   1. kommer. 2. talar. 3. arbetar. 4. behöver. 5. läser 6. tror.

II.   1. Jag har bokat ett rum.
      2. Är du herr Andersson?
      3. Trevligt att träffas.
      4. Ursäkta mig, var ligger hotellet?
      5. Skulle du vilja ha en kopp kaffe?

III. 1. arbetade
      2. behövde
      3. bokade
      4. hette
      5. träffade
      6. talade

IV.   1. Jag ska inte gå.
      2. Jag måste skriva till henne.
      3. Du kommer att behöva det imorgon. (*Du ska behöva det imorgon* is
         acceptable)
      4. Han skulle läsa men han kan inte.
      5. Det behövdes av mig.

V.   1. sov
      2. kom
      3. skrev
      4. band
      5. fann

VI.   1. har talat
      2. har kommit
      3. har skrivit
      4. har trott
      5. har läst
      6. har ringt

VII.   1. Boken behövs av mig.
       2. Den skrevs av dig.
       3. Det har trotts av alla.
       4. Det läses av henne.

Lesson 3

I.   1. min
       2. ditt *or* ert
       3. hans
       4. deras
       5. hennes
       6. vår

II.   1. stort
       2. trött
       3. ny
       4. dyrt
       5. gott

III.   1. Jag skulle vilja ha ett glas vin.
       2. Vi har beställt bord.
       3. Jag skulle vilja ha fisken.
       4. Jag skulle vilja ha en kopp kaffe.
       5. Ursäkta mig, men skulle jag kunna få notan?
       6. Hur mycket kostar det?

IV.   1. stora
       2. trötta
       3. nya
       4. dyra
       5. goda

       1. What is your name?
       2. Have you decided then?
       3. Something to drink?
       4. Would you like anything else?
       5. Would you like the check?

Lesson 4

I.
1. åtta
2. sjutton
3. femhundratrettiofyra
4. sjuhundratjugosex
5. etttusentrehundrafyrtiotvå
6. enmiljontvåhundratrettiofyratusensexhundrasjuttiotvå

II.
1. Klockan är tio.
2. Klockan är tjugo över elva.
3. Klockan är fem i halv ett.
4. Klockan är fem över halv två.
5. Klockan är tjugo i fem.
6. Klockan är kvart i sex.

III.
1. Första januari
2. Tredje februari
3. Fjortonde mars
4. Tjugoandra juni
5. Tjugoåttonde augusti
6. Trettioförsta december

IV.
1. Jag skulle vilja se alla viktiga ställen.
2. Hur kommer man till Stadshuset?
3. Var kan vi sitta och ta en kopp kaffe?
4. Har du en karta över stan?
5. Finns det en rundtur i stan?

V.
1. It is a kilometer.
2. Walk straight ahead and turn to the left.
3. There is a city boat tour.
4. It is a little far to walk.
5. The museum is open at two o'clock.

Lesson 5

I.   1. konstigt
      2. krokigt
      3. svårt
      4. snabbt
      5. trevligt

II.   1. dit
      2. ute
      3. hem
      4. inne
      5. upp
      6. var

III. 1. aldrig
      2. då
      3. redan
      4. någonsin
      5. verkligen
      6. ännu

IV.   1. Jag har gått vilse.
      2. Kan du säga mig hur man kommer till Kungliga slottet?
      3. Är det långt?
      4. Hur kommer jag dit?
      5. Jag försöker hitta Fiskekyrkan.

V.   1. It is near the church in the Old Town.
      2. The street changes name to Stream Street.
      3. Now you are at *Storkyrkan* (the Great Church).
      4. Just go out of this door and you are on Merchant Street.
      5. If you want to buy good fish, I can suggest the Merchant Hall.

Lesson 6

I. 1. konstigare
    2. större
    3. lättare
    4. snabbare
    5. yngre

II. 1. starkare, starkaste.
    2. sämre, sämsta
    3. mognare, mognaste
    4. enklaste
    5. mer irriterad, mest irriterad

III. 1. tycker
     2. tror
     3. tror
     4. tänk
     5. tänk
     6. tror

IV. 1. kan
    2. vet
    3. känner
    4. känner
    5. kan
    6. vet

V. 1. Det finns så mycket att se här.
    2. Jag skulle vilja köpa ett par skor.
    3. Det är för dyrt. Har du någonting billigare?
    4. Jag skulle vilja prova den här tröjan.
    5. Jag tycker om den här. Jag skulle vilja köpa den.

VI. 1. Do you like Sweden?
    2. What do you want to shop for?
    3. There are sweaters in this store.
    4. Does it suit you? *or* Does it fit?
    5. What size do you take?

Lesson 7

I. 1. av
2. i
3. efter
4. från *or* ifrån
5. om
6. med
7. åt
8. vid

II. 1. i
2. om
3. i våras
4. igår
5. i vår
6. i morgon
7. i onsdags

III. 1. sitt *or* sina (since the words can be singular or plural)
2. hennes
3. sin
4. deras
5. sitt *or* sina (since the words can be singular or plural)
6. deras

IV. 1. hennes
2. sin
3. hans
4. hennes
5. hennes, sitt *or* sina (since the words can be singular or plural)

V. 1. gånger
2. tid
3. tid
4. gånger
5. gånger

VI. 1. Förlåt att jag är försenad.
2. Trevligt att träffas.
3. Var kan jag köpa några vykort?
4. Har du (ni) några frimärken?
5. Ja skulle vilja presentera dig för Herr Berg.

VII. 1. Would you like a glass of wine?
2. Would you like to have coffee?
3. You can send an e-mail from here.
4. We do not have any telephone cards.
5. We are out of stamps.

Lesson 8

I. 1. var
2. där
3. var
4. där
5. där

II. 1. därför att
2. eftersom
3. tills
4. för att
5. fast *or* fastän

III. 1. eller
2. för
3. men
4. och

IV. 1. trevligast
2. bäst
3. oftare
4. närmare
5. mer

V.   1. Är du redo för mötet?
       2. Har du kontrollerat datorn?
       3. Är du nervös?
       4. Du borde ha kontrollerat batteriet.
       5. Har du en mobiltelefon?

VI.   1. I have made the copies.
       2. We have no computer. *or* We don't have a computer.
       3. I am not going to be there today. *or* I will not be there today.
       4. One gets five weeks of vacation in Sweden.
       5. You have been very helpful.

Lesson 9

I.   1. lärt sig
      2. klippa mig
      3. rak dig
      4. känner dig
      5. skynda sig

II.   1. träffa
      2. träffas
      3. ses
      4. ser
      5. tycker
      6. tycks

III. 1. skrivande
      2. köpande
      3. pratande
      4. troende
      5. boende
      6. ätande

      1. drucken/drucket/druckna
      2. frågad/frågat/frågade
      3. förlåten/förlåtet/förlåtna

4. hjälpt/hjälpt/hjälpta
5. kommen/kommet/komna
6. trodd/trott/trodda

V. 1. Jag skulle vilja klippa mig.
    2. Vad behöver vi till middag?
    3. Hur mycket kostar det att permanenta mig?
    4. Vilket slags vin skulle du vilja ha till middag?
    5. Skulle jag kunna få manikyr?

VI. 1. You can buy wine at Systembolaget.
    2. We have no pasta in this store.
    3. What color do you want to color your hair?
    4. You would look good as a blond.
    5. I cannot recommend that.

Lesson 10

I.   1. Han har aldrig varit i Sverige.
     2. Jag vill inte köpa en platsbiljett.
     3. Jag går alltid till affären.
     4. Hon köper sällan pasta.
     5. Kommer du ofta hit?

II. 1. Jag tror att jag inte ska träffa honom imorgon.
     2. Jag tror att vi inte äter hemma.
     3. Jag tror att du inte har sett honom.
     4. Jag tror att hon inte sitter under bordet.
     5. Jag tror att han inte är bra.
     6. Jag tror att han aldrig har varit i Sverige.

III. 1. Idag skriver jag.
     2. Igår köpte jag böckerna.
     3. Nu måste du åka hem.
     4. I förrgår har hon kommit hem.
     5. Imorgon ska han åka till Sverige.
     6. Nu äter vi.

IV. 1. Jag skulle vilja ha en biljett till Malmö.
2. Hur dags går nästa tåg till Stockholm?
3. Behöver jag pass att resa till Köpenhamn?
4. Jag skulle vilja ha en andraklass biljett till Göteborg.
5. Var ligger järnvägsstationen?

V. 1. The train goes at five o'clock.
2. You may not rent a car here.
3. You must have a ticket.
4. What sort of car do you want?
5. I need to see your driver's license.

SWEDISH
ENGLISH
VOCABULARY

affär 3 *n. com.*	ahff**eh**r	store/business
affärskontakt 3 *n. com.*	ahff**eh**rskohnt**ah**kt	business contact
affärskvarter 5 *n. neu.*	ahff**eh**rshkvahrtehr	business district
affärskvinna 1 *n. com.*	ahff**eh**rshk**v**innah	businesswoman
affärsman (*pl.* män) *n. com.*	ahff**eh**rshmaahn	businessman
afton (*pl. aftnar*) *n. com.*	**ah**ftohn	evening
alla *pro.*	**ah**llah	everyone
allmän *adj.*	ahllm**eh**n	general/common
allt *pro.*	ahllt	everything
ambassad 3 *n. com.*	ahmbahss**ah**d	embassy
amerikan 3 *n. com.*	ahmehrik**ah**nehn	American
amerikansk *adj.*	ahmehrik**ah**nsk	American
andra *adj.*	**ah**ndrah	other
ankomst 3 *n. com.*	**ah**nkohmst	arrival
annan *adj.*	**ah**nahn	another
arbetare (*pl.* -are) *n. com.*	**ah**rbehtahreh	worker
arbetskostnad 3 *n. com.*	**ah**rbehtskohstnaad	labor costs
Arlanda	**ah**rlahndah	Stockholm airport
att *conj.*	ahtt	that
att (*inf.* particle)	ahtt	to
automat 3 *n. com.*	aaewtohm**aa**t	automat
av *prep.*	aav	by/of
av *adv.*	aav	off
avsluta I *v.*	**aa**vslewtah	finish
bara *adv.*	b**aa**rah	only
batteri 3 *n. neu.*	bahttehr**ee**	battery
be IV (ber-bad-bett) *v.*	beh	ask
behöva IIa *v.*	behh**u**rvah	need
beskriva i-e-e *v.*	behsk**ee**vah	describe
beställa *v.*	behst**eh**llah	reserve
bestämma sig IIa *v. (ref.)*	behst**eh**mmah say	decide
bestämma *v.*	behst**eh**mmah	decide
besök 5 *n. neu.*	behs**er**k	visit
betala I *v.*	beht**ah**lah	pay
bibliotek 5 *n. neu.*	b024blioht**eh**k	library
biffstek 2 *n. com.*	**bi**ffstayk	beef steak
bil 2 *n. com.*	beel	car

bilexpedit 3 *n. com.*	beelehkspehd**ee**t	car agent
biljett 3 *n. com.*	bil**yeh**t	ticket
billig *adj.*	b**i**lleeg	cheaper
biologi 3 *n. com.*	biohlohg**ee**	biology
bjuden *adj.*	by**we**dehn	invited
bli V (blir-blev-blivit) *v.*	blee	become
blond *adj.*	blohnd	blond
blå *adj.*	bl**oa**	blue
blåsa IIb	bl**oa**sah	blow
bo III *v.*	boo	live
boka I *v.*	b**oo**kah	book/reserve
bord 5 *n. neu.*	bohrd	table
borde *v. see* böra	b**oh**rdeh	should
bort *adv.* (*dir.*)	bohrt	away
borta *adv. (loc.)*	b**oh**rtah	away
bra *adj.*; *adv.*	braa	good/well
brandgul *adj.*	br**ah**ndgewl	orange
bredvid *prep.*	brehv**ee**d	next to
bro 2 *n. com.*	broo	bridge
bror (*also* broder *pl.* bröder) *com.*	broor	brother
brun *adj.*	brewn	brown
bröd 5 *n. neu.*	brerrd	bread
buss 2 *n. com.*	buss	bus
byta IIb *v.*	b**iw**tah	change
båda *adj.*	b**ao**dah	both
böra V (bör-borde-bort) *v.*	b**e**r**r**ah	ought
börja I *v.*	b**e**r**r**jah	begin
central *adj.*	sentraal	central
centrum 5 *n. neu.*	s**eh**ntrum	downtown
chaufför 3 *n. com.*	shohff**err**	chauffeur
checka in I *v.*	sh**eh**kkah in	check in
dam 2 *n. com.*	daam	lady
datorkunskap 5 *n. neu.*	d**ah**tohrkunskahp	computer science
de *pron.*	dohm	they
dela ut I *v.*	d**eh**lah ewt	give out
den *pro. com.*	dehn	it

den *art.*	dehn	the
dess *pro.*	dehss	its
det *pro. neu.*	day	it
det *art. neu.*	day	the
det finns	deh finns	there is/are
din *pro.*	deen	your
diskutera I *v.*	diskut**ay**rah	discuss
dit *adv.* (*dir.*)	deet	there
dricka IV i-a-u *v.*	drickah	drink
drink 2 *n. com.*	drink	alcoholic drink
drottning 2 *n. com.*	**droh**ttning	queen
du *sing.*	dew	you
dygnsrytm 3 *n. com.*	dingnsritm	jet lag
dyr *adj.*	diwrt	expensive
då *adv.*	doa	then
där *adv.* (*loc.*)	daehr	there
dörr 2 *n. com.*	derrr	door
efter *prep.*	**eh**ftehr	after
eftermiddag 2 *n. com.*	ehftehrmiddah	afternoon
efterrätt 3 *n. com.*	**eh**ftehr**reh**tt	dessert
efteråt *adv.*	ehftehr**oat**	afterwards
egen *adj.*	**ay**gehn	own
egen hand	**ay**gehn haand	on one's own
ekonomi 3 *n. com.*	ehkohnohnm**ee**	economy
eller *conj.*	**eh**llehr	or
en *com.*	ehn	one/a
enda (enda-enda- enda) *adj.*	**eh**ndah	sole/only
enkel *adj.*	**eh**nkehl	single
e-post 3 *n. com.*	**ay**pohst	e-mail
erbjuda IV u-ö-u *v.*	ayrb**yew**dah	offer
expedit 3 *n. com.*	ehkspehd**eet**	sales clerk
fabrik 3 *n. com.*	fahbrik	factory
far (*also* fader *pl.* fäder) *n. com.*	faar	father
fika I *v.*	**fee**kah	have coffee
fin *adj.*	fin	fine/great

finnas IV i-a-u *v.*	finnahs	exist
fint *adv.*	fint	fine
fira I *v.*	feerah	celebrate
fisk 2 *n. com.*	fisk	fish
fler *adj.*	flayr	many
flyg 5 *n. neu.*	fliwgg	plane
flygplats 3 *n. com.*	fliwgplahts	airport
flygresa 1 *n. com.*	fliwggraysah	plane trip
fortsätta IV ä-a-ä *v.*	fohrtsehttah	continue
frakt 3 *n. com.*	frahkt	postage
fram *adv.* (*dir.*)	frahm	forward
framme *adv.* (*loc.*)	frahmmeh	forward
framtid 3 *n. com.*	frahmteed	future
fransk *adj.*	frahnsk	French
frimärke 4 *n. neu.*	freemehrkeh	stamp
frisör 3 *n. com.*	freeserr	barber
fru 2 *n. com.*	frew	Mrs./Ms./wife
frukost 3 *n. com.*	frukohst	breakfast
fråga I *v.*	fraoga	ask
från *prep.*	fraon	from
fungera I *v.*	fungehrah	work/function
fysik 3 *n. com.*	fiwsik	physics
få IV (får-fick-fått) *v.*	foa	get
få *adj.*	foa	few
färdigt *adj.*	fehrdeet	finished
färg 2 *n. com.*	fehry	color
färga I *v.*	fehrya	color
följa IIa *v.*	ferlyah	follow
för *adv.*	ferr	too
för *prep.*	ferr	for
förbi *adv.*	ferrbee	past
föredra (~drar-~drog- ~dragit) *v.*	ferrehdrah	prefer
föreslå III *v.*	ferrehsloa	suggest
förlåta IV å-ä-å *v.*	ferrloatah	try
förmodligen *adv.*	furrmohdleegehn	probably
förra *adv.*	ferrrah	before/previous
förrän *conj.*	ferrrehn	until

försenad *adj.*	ferrsh**eh**naad	late
förstå III *v.*	ferrsht**oa**	understand
försäkring 2 *n. com.*	fehrsh**eh**kreeng	insurance
försöka IIb *v.*	ferrsh**er**kah	try
förtulla I *v.*	ferrt**u**llah	declare
förälder (*pl.* föräldrar) *n. com.*	ferr**eh**ldehr	parent
gaffel (*pl.* gafflar) *n. com.*	g**ah**ffehl	fork
galleria 1 *n. com.*	g**ah**llehr**ee**ah	shopping mall
gata 1 *n. com.*	g**aa**tah	street
genom *prep.*	y**eh**nohm	through
geografi 3 *n. com.*	yehohgrahf**ee**	geography
glad *adj.*	glaad	glad
glas 5 *n. neu.*	glaas	glass
glasbruk 5 *n. neu.*	gl**aa**sbrewk	glassworks
glassats 3 *n. com.*	gl**aa**ssahts	set of glasses
god *adj.*	goo	good
godtagbar *adj.*	g**oo**dtaagbahr	acceptable
grå *adj.*	groa	gray
grön *adj.*	grern	green
gud 2 *n. com.*	gewd	God
gul *adj.*	gewl	yellow
gå V (går-gick-gått) *v.*	gao (yik-gohtt)	walk
gå vilse *v. see* gå	goa v**i**lseh	get lost
gång 3 *n. com.*	gohng	time
gård 3 *n. com.*	gohrd	garden
gärna *adv.*	y**eh**rnah	willingly
gäst 3 *n. com.*	yehst	guest
ha V (har-hade-haft)*v.*	haa	have
hallå *intj.*	hahll**oa**	hello
halva *adj.*	h**ah**lvah	half
hamn 2 *n. com.*	hahmn	harbor
han *pro.*	hahn	he
hand (*pl.* händer) *n. com.*	hahnd	hand
handel 2 *n. com.*	h**ah**ndehl	business
handla I *v.*	h**ah**ndlah	shop

hej då *intj.*	hay dao	good-bye
hel *adj.*	hayl	whole
helst *adv.*	hehlst	preferably
hem 5 *n. neu.*	hehm	home
henne *pro.*	he**h**nneh	her
historia 1 *n. com.*	hist**oo**reeah	history
hit *adv. dir.*	heet	here
hitta I *v.*	hitah	find
hjälp 4 *n. neu.*	yehlp	help
hjälpa IIb *v.*	**yeh**lpah	help
hjälpsam *adj.*	**yeh**lpsahm	helpful
hon *pro.*	hoon	she
honung 2 *n. com.*	ho**h**nung	honey
hoppas I *v.*	ho**h**ppahs	hope
hos *prep.*	hoos	at (at someone's house)
hotell 5 *n. neu.*	hoht**eh**ll	hotel
hungrig *adj.*	h**u**ngrig	hungry
hur dags	hewr dahks	at what time
hur *inter.*	hewr	how
hus 5 *n. neu.*	hews	house
hyra I *v.*	hirah	rent
hyrespris 5 *n. neu.*	hirehsprees	cost to rent
hålla IV å-ö-å *v.*	ho**h**llah	hold
hår 5 *n. neu.*	hoar	hair
hälsa I *v.*	he**h**lsah	greet
hälsa på *v.*	he**h**lsah poa	visit (person)
hämta I *v.*	he**h**mtah	fetch
här *adv. loc.*	hehr	here
hög *adj.*	herg	high
höger *adv.*	he**r**gehr	right
höger *adj.*	he**r**gehr	right
högt *adv.*	herkt	highly
höra IIa *v.*	hu**rr**ah	hear
hörn 5 *n. neu.*	herrn	corner
i *prep.*	ee	in
i alla fall *adv.*	ee **ah**llah fahll	anyway
idag *adv.*	eed**aa**	today
idé 3 *n. com.*	eed**ay**	idea

igen *adv.*	iyehn	again
igenom *prep.*	eeyehnohm	in through
imorse *adv.*	eemohrshe	this morning
import 3 *n. com.*	impohrt	import
in *adv.*	in	inside
information 3 *n. com.*	infohrmaashoon	information
ingen *pro.*	ingehn	no one
ingen *adj.*	ingehn	no
ingenting 5 *n. neu.*	ingehnting	nothing
innan *prep.*	innahn	before
inrikes *adv.*	inreekehs	domestic
internationell *adj.*	intehrnahshoonehll	international
istället *adv.*	eestehlleht	instead
ja *intj.*	jaa	yes
jag *pro.*	yaag	I
jo *intj.*	joo	yes
jubileum (*pl.* jubiléer) *n. neu.*	jubilehum	anniversary
järnvägsstation 3 *n. com.*	jehrnvaygstahshoon	railroad station
kafé (*pl.* kaféer) *n. neu.*	kaafay	café
kaffe 5 *n. neu.*	kahffeh	coffee
kall *adj.*	kahl	cold
kalla I *v.*	kahllah	call
kallas I *v.*	kahllahs	be called
kan *v. see* kunna	kahn	can
kanal 2 *n. com.*	kahnahl	canal
kanske *adv.*	kahnsheh	maybe
karta 1 *n. com.*	kahrtah	map
kemi 3 *n. com.*	shehmee	chemistry
ketchup 3 *n. com.*	kehchup	ketchup
kilometer *n. neu.*	keelohmaytehr *or* sheeohmaytehr	kilometer
kiosk 2 *n. com.*	sheeohsk	stand/booth
klar *adj.*	klaar	ready/finished/clear
klass 3 *n. com.*	klahss	class
klippa sig I *v.*	klippah say	have one's hair cut
klippning 2 *n. com.*	klippning	haircut
klocka 1 *n. com.*	klohkkah	clock

kniv 2 *n. com.*	kniv	knife
kolla I *v*	ko**h**llah	check
komma IV o-o-o *v.*	ko**h**mmah	come
komma ihåg *v.*	ko**h**mmah ee**h**o**a**g	remember
see komma		
kommentar 3 *n. com.*	ko**h**mmehnt**aar**	comment
kompis 2 *n. com.*	ko**h**mpees	friend
konserthus 5 *n. neu.*	ko**h**ns**e**hrhews	concert hall
konstig *adj.*	ko**h**nstig	strange
konstmuseum *n.*	ko**h**nstmewsehum	art museum
see museum		
kontrakt 5 *n. neu.*	ko**h**ntr**ah**kt	contract
kontraktvillkor 5 *n. neu.*	ko**h**ntr**ah**ktvillkoar	contract conditions
kontroll 3 *n. com.*	ko**h**ntro**h**ll	control
kontrollera I *v.*	ko**h**ntrohlehrah	check
kopia 1 *n. com.*	ko**h**pe**e**ah	copy
kopp 2 *n com.*	ko**h**pp	cup
korg 2 *n. com.*	ko**h**ry	cart
kosta I *v.*	ko**h**stah	cost
kostnad 3 *n. com.*	ko**h**stnahd	cost
kreditkort 4 *n. neu.*	krehd**ee**tkohrt	credit card
krokig *adj.*	kr**oo**kig	winding
krona 1 *n. com.*	kr**oo**nah	crown
kul (undeclineable,	kewl	cool/fun
slang) *adj.*		
kung 2 *n. com.*	kung	king
kunglig *adj.*	kunglig	royal
kunna V (kan-kunde-	ku**n**nah	be able
kunnat) *v.*		
kvarter 3 *n. com.*	kvahrt**e**hr	block/quarter
kvinna 1 *n. com.*	kvinnah	woman
kväll 2 *n. com.*	kvehll	evening
kyrka 1 *n. com.*	ki**w**rkah	church
kyrkogård 3 *n. com.*	shi**w**rkohgohrd	cemetery
köpa IIb *v.*	sh**e**rpah	buy
körkort 5 *n. neu.*	sh**e**rrkoort	driver's license
kött 5 *n. neu.*	shertt	meat
köttfärs 3 *n. com.*	sh**e**rttfehrsh	hamburger

laga I *v.*	la**a**gah	fix
le (ler-log-lett) *v.*	lay	smile
ledig *adj.*	la**y**deeg	unoccupied
leta efter I *v.*	la**y**tah **eh**ftehr	search for
ligga V (ligger-låg legat) *v.*	li**gg**ah	lie
lik *adj.*	leek	like/similar
lila *adj.*	leelah	purple
lista 1 *n. com.*	li**s**tah	list
lite *adv.*	lee**t**eh	a little
liten (litet-små) *adj.*	lee**t**ehn	little
litteratur 3 *n. com.*	litehrat**ewr**	literature
livstid 3 *n. com.*	li**v**steed	lifetime
ljus *adj.*	yews	light
lunch 3 *n. com.*	lunch	lunch
låg *adj.*	loag	low
lång *adj.*	lo**h**ngg	long
långt *adv.*	lo**h**ngkt	long
låta IV å-ä-å *v.*	la**o**tah	sound
låta IV å-ä-å *v.*	lo**a**tah	allow/let
lägga V (lägger-la(de)-lagt) *v.*	le**h**ggah	put/lay
lämna I *v.*	le**h**mnah	leave
länge *adv.*	le**h**ngeh	long (time)
längs *adv.*	le**h**nks	along
läsa IIb *v.*	le**h**sah	read
lättöl 5 *n. neu.*	le**h**tterl	light beer
löna sig *v.*	le**r**naa say	to be worthwhile
man (*pl.* män) *n. com.*	mahn	man
man (*pl.* män) *n. com.*	mahn	husband
man *pro.*	mahn	one
manikyr 3 *n. com.*	mahnik**ir**	manicure
marknad 3 *n. com.*	ma**h**rknahd	market
matematik 3 *n. com.*	mahtehmaht**eek**	mathematics
med *prep.*	may	with
medarbetare (*pl.* -are) *n. com.*	ma**y**dahrbehtahreh	co-worker
meddela I *v.*	ma**y**ddehlah	inform

medicin 3 *n. com.*	mehdis**een**	medicine
men *conj.*	mehn	but
meny (*pl.* menyer) *n. neu.*	mehn**iw**	menu
mer *adj.*	mehr	more
middag 2 *n. com.*	**mi**ddah	dinner
middag 2 *n. com.*	**mi**ddah	afternoon
midnattsol 2 *n. com.*	**mi**ddnahtts**ool**	midnight sun
mig *pro.*	may	me
min *pro.*	min	mine/my
mindre *adj.*	**mi**ndreh	smaller
minut 3 *n. com.*	min**ewt**	minute
mjölk 2 *n. com.*	my**erlk**	milk
mobiltelefon 3 *n. com.*	moh**bee**ltehlehfoan	cell phone
mor (*pl.* mödrar) *n. com.*	moor	mother
morgon (*pl.* morgnar) *n. com.*	**moh**rrohn	morning
museum 3 (*pl.* muséer) *n. neu.*	mews**eh**um	museum
mycket *adv.*	**mi**wkeh	much
många *adj.*	**mo**angah	many
måste V (måste-måste-måst) *v.*	**moh**steh	must
människa 1 *n. com.*	**meh**nnishah	person (*pl.* people)
märka IIb *v.*	**meh**rkah	notice
möte 4 *n. neu.*	**mu**rteh	meeting
namn 5 *n. neu.*	nahmn	name
namnkort 5 *n. neu.*	**nah**mnkohrt	name card
nationell *adj.*	nashoon**ehl**	national
natt (*pl.* nätter) *n. com.*	naht	night
naturligtvis *adv.*	naht**ew**rlitvees	naturally
ner *adv.* (*dir.*)	nehr	down
nere *adv.*(*loc.*)	**neh**reh	down
nervös *adj.*	nehrv**urs**	nervous
nog *adv.*	noog	probably/I expect to
Norden	**noh**rdehn	Nordic Countries
normal *adj.*	nohrm**aal**	normal
nota 1 *n. com.*	**noo**tah	check/bill

nu *adv.*	new	now
nummer 5 *n. neu.*	n**u**mmehr	number
nyfiken *adj.*	n**iw**feekehn	curious
nå *intj.*	noa	well
någon *adj.*	noan *or* n**ao**gohn	some
någon *pro.*	noan *or* n**ao**gohn	someone
någonstans *adv.*	n**ao**nstahns	someplace
någonting 5 *n. neu.*	n**oa**nting	something
nära *adv.*	n**ae**hrah	near
närmaste *adj.*	m**eh**rmahsteh	nearest
nästa *adj.*	n**eh**stah	next
nästan *adv.*	n**eh**staan	almost
nät 5 *n. neu.*	neht	Internet/Net
nödvändig *adj.*	n**er**dvehndig	necessary
nöje 4 *n. neu.*	n**ur**yeh	pleasure
nöjespark 2 *n. com.*	n**er**yehspahrk	amusement park
och *conj.*	oh *or* ohk	and
också *adv.*	**oh**ksoh	also
okej *intj.*	ohk**ay**	ok
olja 1 *n. com.*	**oh**lyah	oil
om *prep.*	ohm	about
om *conj.*	ohm	if
operahus 5 *n. neu.*	**oh**pehrahhews	opera house
orsak 3 *n. com.*	**oh**rshaak	reason
otroligt *adv.*	ohtr**oo**lit	unbelievable
papper 5 *n.neu.*	p**ah**ppehr	paper
par 5 *n. neu.*	paar	pair
park 3 *n. com.*	pahrk	park
pass 5 *n. neu.*	pahss	passport
passa I *v.*	p**ah**ssah	suit
passkontroll 3 *n. com.*	pahsskohtr**oh**ll	passport control
pasta 1 *n. com.*	p**ah**stah	pasta
permanenta sig I *v.*	pehrmahn**eh**ntah say	have a perm
personal 3 *n. com.*	pehrshohn**ah**l	personnel
pizza 1 *n. com.*	p**i**tssah	pizza
placerad *adj.*	pla**a**sehrahd	placed
plan 5 *n. neu.*	pl**aa**h	level
plats 3 *n. com.*	plahts	square/place

post 3 *n. com.*	pohst	mail
postlåda *n. com.*	pohstloadah	mailbox
prata I *v.*	praatah	talk
precis *adv.*	prehsees	exactly
presentation 3 *n. com.*	prehsehntahshoon	presentation
presentera I *v.*	prehsehntayrah	present
pris 3 *n. com.*	prees	price
problem 5 *n. neu.*	prohblehm	problem
procent 5 *n. com.*	prohsehnt	percent
produktivitet 5 *n. neu.*	prohduktiviteht	productivity
promenad 3 *n. com.*	prohmehnaad	walk
prova I *v.*	proovah	try out/on
på *prep.*	pao	on
pågå V (~går-~gick- ~gått) *v.*	paogao	going on
pärm 2 *n. com.*	pehrm	folder
rabatt 3 *n. com.*	rahbahtt	rebate
rakt *adv.*	raakt	straight
rakt fram *adv.*	rahkt frahm	straight ahead
rea 1 *n. com.*	rayah	sale
reception 3 *n. com.*	rehsehpshoon	reception
redan *adv.*	raydahn	already
redo *adj.*(undeclinable)	raydao	ready
regna I *v.*	rehgnah	rain
rekommendera I *v.*	rehkohmehndehrah	recommend
resa IIb *v.*	raysah	travel
resecheckar 2 *n. com.*	raysehshehkkahr	traveler's checks
restaurang 3 *n. com.*	restehrahng	restaurant
retur *see* tur		
riksdag 2 *n. com.*	riksdaag	parliament
riktigt *adv.*	riktit	right
ringa IIa *v.*	ringah	call
rock 2 *n. com.*	rohkk	coat
rosa *adj.*	roosah	pink
rubbad *adj.*	rubbahd	upset/dislodged
rum 5 *n. neu.*	rum	room
rundtur 3 *n. com.*	rundtewr	sightseeing tour
runt *adv.*	runt	around

råd *n. neu.*	road	advice
räckvidd *adj.*	rehkkvidd	range
rädd *adj.*	rehdd	afraid
räkning 2 *n. com.*	rehkkning	check/bill
räksmörgås *n. com.*	rehksmerrgoas	shrimp sandwich
röd *adj.*	rerd	red
sak 3 *n. com.*	saak	thing
salt (*pl.* salter) *n. neu.*	sahlt	salt
samma *adj.*	sahmmah	same
se V (ser-såg-sett) *v.*	say	see
sedan *adv.*	saydahn *or* sehn	then/later
semester 2 *n. com*	sehmehstehr	vacation
senap 3 *n. com.*	sehnahp	mustard
senare *adj.*	saynahreh	later
senaste *adj.*	saynahsteh	latest
servett 3 *n. com.*	sehrveht	napkin
servitör 3 *n. com.*	sehrviterr	waiter
ses V (ses-sågs-setts) *v.*	says	see each other *or* be seen
se ut *v. see* se	say ewt	look (like)
sida 1 *n. com.*	seedah	side
sig *pro.*	say	himself/herself
sin *pro.*	seen	his/her own
sist *adj.*	sist	last
sitta IV i-a-u *v.*	sittah	sit
sjukförsäkring 2 *n. com.*	shewkferrrshehkring	health insurance
ska *v.*	skah	will
skatt 3 *n. neu.*	skahtt	tax
sked 2 *n. com.*	shehd	spoon
skeppskaj 3 *n. com.*	shehpskahy	ship quay
skicka I *v.*	shikkah	send
skina IV i-e-i *v.*	shinah	shine
sko (*pl.* skor) *n. com.*	skoo	shoe
skriva IV i-e-i *v.*	skreevah	write
skulle *v.*	skulleh	would
skål *intj.*	skoal	cheers
skärgård 2 *n. com.*	shehrgohrd	archipelago
slags 5 *n. neu.*	slahks	sort

slott 5 *n. neu.*	slohtt	castle
slut *adj.*	slewt	end
slut 5 *n. com.*	slewt	finish/end
sluta I *v.*	slewtah	stop/finish
slösa I *v.*	slursah	while away/waste
smör 5 *n. neu.*	smerr	butter
snabbt *adv.*	snahbt	quickly
snart *adv.*	snahrt	soon
snäll *adj.*	snehll	nice
snälla I *v.*	snehllah	be nice
snö (no plural) *n. com.*	sner	snow
snöa I *v.*	snerah	snow
socker 5 *n. neu.*	sohkkehr	sugar
som *pron.*	sohm	who
som *conj.*	sohm	as
sort 3 *n. com.*	sohrt	sort
sova IV o-o-o *v.*	sohvah	sleep
sova middag *v. see* sova	sohvah midah	take a nap
spara I *v.*	spaarah	save
speciell *adj.*	spehseeehll	special
stad (*pl.* städer) *n. com.*	staad	city
stadsbåttur 3 *n. com.*	stahtsboattewr	city boat tour
stadscentrum 5 *n. neu.*	stahtssehntrum	downtown
stan *see* stad	staan	the city
stanna I *v.*	stahnnah	stay
stiga IV i-e-i *v.*	steegah	get in
stoppa I *v.*	stohppah	put/stuff
stor *adj.*	stoor	big
storlek 2 *n. com.*	stoorlehk	size
strand 3 *n. com.*	strahnd	shore/beach
strunta I *v.*	struntah	ignore
stund 3 *n. com.*	stund	moment
stå III *v.*	stoa	stand
ställa IIa *v.*	stehllah	place
ställe 4 *n. neu.*	stehlleh	place
surfa I *v.*	surfah	surf
svart *adj.*	svahrt	black
svensk *adj.*	svehnsk	Swedish

svenska *n.*	svehnskah	Swedish (language)
Sverige *n. com.*	svehreeyeh	Sweden
svår *adj.*	svoar	difficult
svänga IIa *v.*	svehngah	turn
synd *adj.*	siwnd	too bad/pity
Systembolaget	sistaymboolaageht	State liquor store
syster (*pl.* systrar) *n. com.*	siwstehr	sister
så *adv.*	soa	so
säga V (säger-sa-sagt) *v.*	sehya	say
säkert *adv.*	saykehrt	certainly
sätt 5 *n. neu.*	sehtt	way/manner
sätta upp V (sätter-satte-satt) *v.*	sehttaa upp	set up
ta V (tar-tog-tagit) *v.*	taa	take
tack 4 *n. neu.*	tahkk	thanks
tacka I *v.*	tahkkah	thank
tag 5 *n. neu.*	taag	ahold
tala I *v.*	taalah	speak
tandkräm *n. com.*	tahndkraym	toothpaste
taxi (*pl.* taxi) *n. com.*	tahksee	taxi
teater (*pl.* teatrar) *n. com.*	tehahtehr	theater
telefon 3 *n. com.*	tehlehfohn	telephone
telefonkort 5 *n. neu.*	tehlehfohnkohrt	telephone card
tid 3 *n. com.*	teed	time
till *prep.*	till	to
till bords	till bohrds	to the table
tillbaka *adv.*	tillbaakah	back
tills *conj.*	tills	until
tillsammans *adv.*	tillsahmmahns	together
titta I *v.*	tittah	look
titta på *v.*	tittah poa	look at
tjaa *intj.*	chaah	well
tjänst 3 *n. com.*	shehnst	service
toalettpapper 5 *n. neu.*	tohahlehtpahppehr	toilet paper
torg 5 *n. neu.*	tohry	square
torsk 2 *n. com.*	tohrshk	cod

trevlig *adv.*	trehvlig	pleasant
tro III *v.*	troo	believe
tråkig *adj.*	troakig	boring
träffa I *v.*	trehffah	meet
träffas *v.*	trehffahs	meet each other *or* to be met
träskor *n. com.*	trayskoo	clogs
tröja 1 *n. com.*	treryah	sweater
tull 2 *n. com.*	tull	customs
tur och retur *adv.*	tewr o rehtewr	round trip
turistbok (*pl.* -böcker) *n. com.*	tewreestbook	guidebook
turistinformation 3 *n. com.*	tewreestinfohrmahshoon	tourist information
tvättmedel 5 *n. neu.*	tvehttmaydehl	laundry soap
tycka IIb *v.*	tikkah	believe *or* have the opinion
tåg 5 *n. neu.*	toag	train
tågkort 5 *n. neu.*	toagkoort	train card
tågstation 3 *n. com.*	toagstahshoon	train station
tänka IIb *v.*	tehnkah	to think
underlig *adj.*	undehrlig	strange
ung *adj.*	ung	young
ungefär *adv.*	unyehfehr	about *or* approximately
universitet 5 *n. neu.*	univehrshitayt	university
upp *adv.* (*dir.*)	upp	up
uppe *adv.* (*loc.*)	uppeh	up
uppgift 3 *n. com.*	uppyift	information/ instructions
ursäkta I *v.*	ewrshehktah	excuse
USA	ewehsah	USA
ut *adv.* (*dir.*)	ewt	out
utan *conj.*	ewtahn	without
utanför *adv.*	ewtahnferr	outside
utbytesstudent 3 *n. com.*	ewtbiwtehsstewdehnt	exchange student
ute *adv.* (*loc.*)	ewt	out
utrikes *adv.*	ewtreekes	abroad/international
utsida 1 *n. com.*	ewtseedah	exterior

utställning 2 *n. com.*	**ew**tstehlning	exhibition
vacker *adj.*	**vah**kehr	beautiful
vad *inter.*	vah	what
vad *intj.*	vah	how! what!
vaktombyte 4 *n. neu.*	**vah**ktohmb**iw**teh	changing of the guards
vandra I *v.*	**vah**ndrah	wander
vanlig *adj.*	**vaa**nlig	ordinary
var *v. see* vara	vaar	was
var *adv.(loc.)*	vaar	where
vara V (är-var-varit) *v.*	**vaa**rah	be
varje *adj.*	**vah**ryeh	each
varje *pro.*	**vah**ryeh	each person
varm *adj.*	vahrm	warm
varmrätt 3 *n. com.*	**vah**rmreht	main course
varsågod	vahrsoag**oo**	here you are
vart *adv.* (*dir.*)	vahrt	where to
varuhus *n. neu.*	**vaa**rewhews	department store
vecka 1 *n. com.*	**veh**kkah	week
verkligen *adv.*	**veh**rkleegen	really
veta V	**vay**tah	know
(vet-visste-vetat) *v.*		
vetenskap 5 *n. neu.*	**vay**tehnskahp	science
vid *prep.*	veed	at/by
videoapparat 3 *n. com.*	**vee**dehohahppahr**aat**	video machine
viktig *adj.*	**vik**tig	important
vild *adj.*	vild	wild
vilja V (vill-ville-velat) *v.*	**vil**yah	want
vilken *pron.*	**vil**kehn	which
vin (*pl.* viner) *n. neu.*	veen	wine
vinäger 2 *n. com.*	vin**ay**gehr	vinegar
virrvarr 5 *n. neu.*	**vir**rvahrr	muddle/confusion
visa I *v.*	**vee**sah	show
viss *adj.*	viss	course/certain
visst *adv.*	visst	of course
vistelse 3 *n. com.*	**vis**tehlseh	stay
vit *adj.*	vit	white
vore *v. see* vara	**voh**reh	were *v.*
vykort 5 *n. neu.*	**viw**kohrt	postcard

väder 2 *n. com.*	vehdehr	weather
väg 2 *n. com.*	vehg	way/road
väldig *adj.*	vehldeeg	huge
välkommen *adj.*	vaelkohmmehn	welcome
välkomst 3 *n. com.*	vaylkohmst	welcome
vän 3 *n. com.*	vehn	friend
vänlig *adj.*	vehnlig	friendly/nice
vänster *adj.*	vehnstehr	left
vänster *adv.*	vehnstehr	left
väska 1 *n. com.*	vehskah	suitcase/bag
växelkontor 5 *n. com.*	vehksehlkohntoor	exchange office
växelpersonal *n. com.*	vehksehlpehrshohnahl	exchange personnel
växla I *v.*	vehkslah	exchange
åka IIb *v.*	aokah	go (by vehicle)
år 5 *n. neu.*	ohr	year
åt *prep.*	oat	for/at
återkomma IV o-o-o *v.*	oatehrkohmmah	return
ägg 5 *n. neu.*	ehgg	egg
älska I *v.*	ehlskah	love
älv 2 *n.com.*	ehlv	river
än *conj.*	ehn	than (with comparisons)
äntligen *adv.*	ehntleegehn	finally
är *v. see* vara	ehr	am/is/are
äta IV ä-å-ä *v.*	aehtah	eat
ö 2 *n. com.*	er	island
ögonblick 5 *n. neu.*	ergohnblikk	moment
öka I *v.*	erkah	increase
öl 5 *n. neu.*	erl	beer
öppen *adj.*	erppehn	open
östra *adj.*	erstrah	eastern
över *prep.*	ervehr	over

ENGLISH
SWEDISH
VOCABULARY

a/an	en/ett
about *adv.*	ungefär
about *prep.*	om
acceptable *adj.*	godtagbar
advice *n.*	råd
afraid *adj.*	rädd
after *prep.*	efter
afternoon *n.*	eftermiddag 2
afterwards *adv.*	efteråt
again *adv.*	igen
ahold *n. neu.*	tag 5
airport *n.*	flygplats 3
alcoholic drink *n.*	drink 2
allow/let *v.*	låta IV å-ä-å
almost *adv.*	nästan
along *adv.*	längs
already *adv.*	redan
also *adv.*	också
American *n.*	amerikan 3
American *adj.*	amerikansk
amusement park *n.*	nöjespark 2
and *conj.*	och
anniversary *n.*	jubileum (*pl.* jubiléer)
anything *pro.*	något
anyway *adv.*	i alla fall
approximately *adv.*	ungefär
archipelago *n.*	skärgård 2
around *adv.*	runt
arrival *n.*	ankomst 3
art museum *n.*	konstmuseum
as *conj.*	som
ask *v.*	fråga I
at *prep.*	åt/vid
at (at someone's house) *prep.*	hos
at what time	hur dags
automat *n.*	automat 3
away *adv.* (*dir.*)	bort
away *adv.* (*loc.*)	borta

back *adv.*	tillbaka
bag *n.*	väska 1
barber *n.*	frisör 3
battery *n.*	batteri 3
be *v.*	vara V (är-var-varit)
beautiful *adj.*	vacker
become *v.*	bli V (blir-blev-blivit)
beef steak *n.*	biffstek 2
beer *n.*	öl 5
before *adv.*	förra
before *prep.*	innan
begin *v.*	börja I
believe *v.*	tycka IIb *or* tro III
big *adj.*	stor
bill *n.*	nota 1 *or* räkning 2
biology *n.*	biologi 3
black *adj.*	svart
block *n.*	kvarter 3
blond *adj.*	blond
blow *v.*	blåsa IIb
blue *adj.*	blå
book *v.*	boka I
booth *n.*	kiosk 2
boring *adj.*	tråkig
both *adj.*	båda
bread *n.*	bröd 5
breakfast *n.*	frukost 3
bridge *n.*	bro 2
brown *adj.*	brun
bus *n. com.*	buss 2
business *n.*	affär 3 *or* handel 3
business contact *n.*	affärskontakt 3
business district *n.*	affärskvarter 3
businessman *n.*	affärsman (*pl.* män)
businesswoman *n.*	affärskvinna 1
but *conj.*	men
butter *n.*	smör 5

buy *v.*	köpa IIb
by *prep.*	av *or* vid
café *n.*	kafé 5 (-er)
call (be called) *v.*	kallas I
call (by name) *v.*	kalla I
call (on phone) *v.*	ringa IIa
can *v.*	kunna V (kan-kunde-kunnat)
canal *n.*	kanal 2
car *n.*	bil 2
car agent *n.*	bilexpedit 3
cart *n.*	korg 2
castle *n.*	slott 5
celebrate *v.*	fira
cell phone *n.*	mobiltelefon 3
cemetery *n.*	kyrkogård 3
central *adj.*	central
certain *adj.*	visst
certainly *adv.*	säkert
change *v.*	byta IIb
changing of the guards *n.*	vaktombyte 4
chauffeur *n.*	chaufför 3
cheap *adj.*	billig
check *v.*	kontrollera I *or* kolla I
check in *v.*	checka in
cheers *intrj.*	skål
chemistry *n.*	kemi 3
church *n.*	kyrka 1
city *n.*	stad (*pl.* städer)
city boat tour *n.*	stadsbåttur 3
class *n.*	klass 3
clear *adj.*	klar
clock *n.*	klocka 1
clogs *n.*	träskor
coat *n.*	rock 2
cod *n.*	torsk 2
coffee *n.*	kaffe 5
coffee (have coffee) *v.*	fika I
cold *adj.*	kall
color *n.*	färg 2

color *v.*	färga I
come *v.*	komma IV o-o-o
comment *n.*	kommentar 3
common *adj.*	allmän
computer science *n.*	datorkunskap 5
concert hall *n.*	konserthus 5
confusion *n.*	virrvarr 5
continue *v.*	fortsätta IV ä-a-ä
contract *n.*	kontrakt 5
contract conditions *n.*	kontraktvillkor 5
control *n.*	kontroll 3
cool *adj.*	kul (slang)
copy *n.*	kopia 1
corner *n.*	hörn 5
cost *n.*	kostnad 3
cost *v.*	kosta I
co-worker *n.*	medarbetare (*pl.* -are)
credit card *n.*	kreditkort 4
crown *n.*	krona 1
cup *n.*	kopp 2
curious *adj.*	nyfiken
customs *n.*	tull 2
customs personnel *n.*	tullpersonal 3
decide *v.*	bestämma sig IIa
declare *v.*	förtulla
department store	varuhus
describe *v.*	beskriva
dessert *n.*	efterrätt 3
difficult *adj.*	svår
dinner *n.*	middag 2
discuss *v.*	diskutera I
dollar	dollar
domestic *adv.*	inrikes
door *n.*	dörr 2
down *adv.* (*loc.*)	nere
down *adv.* (*dir.*)	ner
downtown *n.*	centrum *or* stadscentrum 5
drink *v.*	dricka IV i-a-u
driver's license *n.*	körkort 5

each *adj.*	varje
each (person) *pro.*	varje
eastern *adj.*	östra
eat *v.*	äta IV ä-å-ä
economy *n.*	ekonomi 3
egg *n.*	ägg 5
e-mail *n.*	epost 3
embassy *n.*	ambassad 3
end *adj.*	slut
end *n.*	slut 5
end *v.*	sluta I
evening *n.*	kväll 2 *or* afton (*pl.* aftnar)
everyone *pro.*	alla
everything *pro.*	allt
exactly *adv.*	precis
exchange *v.*	växla I
exchange office *n.*	växelkontor 5
exchange personnel *n.*	växelpersonal
exchange student *n.*	utbytesstudent 3
excuse *v.*	ursäkta I
exhibition *n.*	utställning 2
exist *v.*	finnas IV i-a-u
expensive *adj.*	dyr
exterior *n.*	utsida 1
factory *n.*	fabrik 3
fetch *v.*	hämta I
few *adj.*	få
finally *adv.*	äntligen
find *v.*	hitta I
find oneself *v.*	befinna sig IV i-a-u
fine *adj.*	fin
fine *adv.*	fint
finish *n.*	slut 5
finish *v.*	sluta I *or* avsluta I
finished *adj.*	klar *or* färdig
fish *n. com.*	fisk 2
fix *v.*	laga I
folder *n.*	pärm 2

follow *v.*	följa IIa
for *prep.*	åt *or* för
forgive *v.*	förlåta IV å-ä-å
fork *n.*	gaffel 2
forward *adv.* (*dir.*)	fram
forward *adv.* (*loc.*)	framme
friend *n.*	kompis 2 *or* vän 3
friendly *adj.*	vänlig
from *prep.*	från
function *v.*	fungera I
future *n.*	framtid 3
garden *n.*	gård 3
general *adj.*	allmän
geography *n.*	geografi 3
get *v.*	få V (får-fick-fått)
get in *v.*	stiga på IV i-e-i
glad *adj.*	glad
glass *n.*	glas 5
glasses (set of glasses) *n.*	glassats 3
glassworks *n.*	glasbruk 5
go (under own power)	gå V (går-gick-gått)
go (by vehicle) *v.*	åka IIb
God *n.*	gud 2
going on *v.*	pågå V (~går-~gick-~gått)
good *adj.*	god *or* bra
good-bye *intj.*	hej då
gray *adj.*	grå
green *adj.*	grön
greet *v.*	hälsa I
guest *n.*	gäst 3
guidebook *n.*	turistbok (*pl.* -böcker)
hair *n.*	hår 5
haircut *n.*	klippning 2
haircut (have one's hair cut) *v.*	klippa sig I
half *adj.*	halva
hamburger *n.*	köttfärs 3
hand *n.*	hand (*pl.* händer)
harbor *n.*	hamn 2

have *v.*	ha V (har-hade-haft)
he *pro.*	han
health insurance *n.*	sjukförsäkring 2
hear *v.*	höra IIa
hello *intj.*	hallå/hej
help *v.*	hjälpa IIb
helpful *adj.*	hjälpsam
her *pro.*	henne
her own *pro.*	sin
here *adv.* (*dir.*)	hit
here *adv.* (loc.)	här
hers *pro.*	hennes
herself (reflexive) *pro.*	sig
high *adj.*	hög
highly *adv.*	högt
himself (reflexive) *pro.*	sig
his *pro.*	hans
his own *pro.*	sin
history *n.*	historia 1
hold *v.*	hålla IV å-ö-å
home *n.*	hem 5
honey *n.*	honung 2
hope *v.*	hoppas I
hotel *n.*	hotell 5
house *n.*	hus 5
how *inter.*	hur
huge *adj.*	väldig
hungry *adj.*	hungrig
husband *n.*	man (*pl.* män)
I *pro.*	jag
idea *n.*	idé 3
if *conj.*	om
ignore *v.*	strunta I
import *n.*	import 3
important *adj.*	viktig
in *prep.*	i
increase *v.*	öka I
inform *v.*	meddela I

information *n.*	uppgift 3 *or* information 3
inside *adv.* (*dir.*)	in
inside *adv.* (*loc.*)	inne
instructions *n.*	uppgift 3
insurance *n.*	försäkring 2
international *adj.*	internationell *or* utrikes
Internet *n.*	internet 5 *or* internät 5 *or* nät 5
invited *adj.*	bjuden
island *n.*	ö 2
it	det/den
jet lag *n.*	dygnsrytm 3
ketchup *n.*	ketchup 3
kilometer *n.*	kilometer 5
king *n.*	kung 2
knife *n.*	kniv 2
know *v.*	veta V (vet-visste-vetat)
labor costs *n.*	arbetskostnad 3
lady *n.*	dam 2
last *adj.*	sist
late *adj.*	försenad
later *adj.*	senare
latest *adj.*	senaste
laundry soap *n.*	tvättmedel 5
lay *v.*	lägga V (lägger-la(de)-lagt)
leave *v.*	lämna I
left *adj.*	vänster
level *n.*	plan 5
library *n.*	bibliotek 5
lie *v.*	ligga V (ligger-låg-legat)
lifetime *n.*	livstid 3
light beer *n.*	lättöl 5
light *adj.*	ljus
like *adj.*	lik
list *n.*	lista 1
literature *n.*	litteratur 3
little *adv.*	lite
little *adj.*	liten (litet-små)
live (at a place) *v.*	bo III

live (exist) *v.*	leva IIa
long (time) *adv.*	länge
long *adv.*	långt
long *adj.*	lång
look at *v.*	titta på I
look *v.*	titta I
look like *v.*	se ut V *see* se
lost (get lost) *v.*	gå vilse
love *v.*	älska I
low *adj.*	låg
lunch *n.*	lunch 3
mail *n.*	post 3
mailbox *n.*	postlåda 1
main course *n.*	varmrätt 3
man *n. com.*	man (män)
manicure *n.*	manikyr 3
manner *n*	sätt 5
many *adj.*	många
many *adj.*	fler
map *n.*	karta 1
market *n.*	marknad 3
mathematics *n.*	matematik 3
maybe *adv.*	kanske
me *pro.*	mig
meat *n.*	kött 5
medicine *n.*	medicin 3
meet *v.*	träffa I
meet each other *v.*	träffas I
meeting *n.*	möte 4
menu *n.*	meny (*pl.* menyer)
midnight sun *n.*	midnattsol 2
milk *n.*	mjölk 2
minute *n.*	minut 3
moment *n.*	ögonblick 5 *or* stund 3
more *adj.*	mer
morning *n.*	morgon (*pl.* morgnar)
mother *n.*	mor (*pl.* mödrar)
Mrs./Ms. *n.*	fru 2

much *adv.*	mycket
muddle *n.*	virrvarr 5
museum *n.*	museum 3 (*pl.* muséer)
must *v.*	måste V (måste-måste-måst)
mustard *n.*	senap 3
my *pro.*	min
name *n. neu.*	namn 5
name card *n.*	namnkort 5
nap (take a nap) *v.*	sova middag
napkin *n.*	servett 3
national *adj.*	nationell
naturally *adv.*	naturligtvis
near *adj.*	nära
nearest *adj.*	närmaste
necessary *adj.*	nödvändig
need *v.*	behöva IIa
nervous *adj.*	nervös
next *adj.*	nästa
next to *prep.*	brevid
nice *adj.*	vänlig
nice *adj.*	snäll
night *n.*	natt (*pl.* nätter)
no one *pro.*	ingen
none *adj.*	ingen
Nordic Countries	norden
normal *adj.*	normal
nothing *n.*	ingenting 5
notice *v.*	märka IIb
now *adv.*	nu
number *n.*	nummer 5
of *prep.*	av
of course *adv.*	visst
offer *v.*	erbjuda IV u-ö-u
oil *n.*	olja 1
ok *intrj.*	okej
on *prep.*	på
one *pro.*	man
only *pro.*	enda (enda-enda-enda)

only *adv.*	endast
only *adv.*	bara
open *adj.*	öppen
opera house *n.*	operahus 5
or *conj.*	eller
orange *adj.*	brandgul
ordinary *adj.*	vanlig
other *adj.*	annan
ought *v.*	böra V (bör-borde-bort)
out (direction) *adv.*	ut
outside *adv.*	utanför
over *prep.*	över
own *adj.*	egen
own *v.*	äga IIa
pair *n.*	par 5
paper *n.*	papper 5
parent *n.*	förälder (*pl.* föräldrar)
park *n.*	park 3
parliament *n.*	riksdag 2
passport *n.*	pass 5
passport control *n.*	Passkontroll 3
past *adv.*	förbi
pasta *n.*	pasta 1
pay *v.*	betala I
people *n.*	människor 1
percent *n.*	procent 5
perm (have a perm) *v.*	permanenta sig I
person *n.*	människa 1
personnel *n. com.*	personal 3
physics *n.*	fysik 3
pink *adj.*	rosa
pity *adj.*	synd
pizza *n.*	pizza 1
place *n.*	plats 3
place *n.*	ställe 4
place *v.*	ställa IIa
placed *adv.*	placed
plane *n.*	flyg 5

plane trip *n.*	flygresa 1
pleasant *adv.*	trevlig
pleasure *n.*	nöje 4
postage *n.*	frakt 3
postcard *n.*	vykort 5
prefer *v.*	föredra
preferably *adv.*	helst
present *v.*	presentera I
presentation *n.*	presentation 3
previous *adv.*	förra
price *n.*	pris 3
probably *adv.*	förmodligen *or* nog
problem *n.*	problem 5
productivity *n.*	produktivitet 5
purple *adj.*	lila
put *v.*	lägga V (lägger-la(de)-lagt)
queen *n.*	drottning 2
quickly *adv.*	snabbt
railroad station *n.*	järnvägsstation 3
rain *v.*	regna I
rain *n.*	regn
range *adj.*	räckvidd
read *v.*	läsa IIb
ready *adj.*	klar *or* redo (undeclineable)
really *adv.*	verkligen
reason *n. com.*	orsak 3
rebate *n.*	rabatt 3
reception *n. com*	reception 3
recommend *v.*	rekommendera I
red *adj.*	röd
remember *v.*	komma ihåg *see* komma
rent *v.*	hyra I
reserve *v.*	boka I *or* beställa IIa
restaurant *n.*	restaurang 3
return *v.*	återkomma IV o-o-o
right *adj.*	höger
right *adv.*	höger
right (correct) *adv.*	riktigt

river *n.*	älv 2
road *n.*	väg 2
room *n.*	rum 5
round trip *adv.*	tur och retur
royal *adj.*	kunglig
sale *n.*	rea 1
sales clerk *n.*	expedit 3
salt *n.*	salt (*pl.* salter)
same *adj.*	samma
save (money) *v.*	spara I
say *v.*	säga V (säger-sa-sagt)
science *n.*	vetenskap 5
search *v.*	leta I
search for *v.*	leta efter I
see *v.*	se V (ser-såg-sett)
see each other	ses
send *v.*	skicka I
service *n.*	tjänst 3
set up *v.*	sätta upp V (sätter-satte-satt)
she *pro.*	hon
shine *v.*	skina IV i-e-i
ship quay *n.*	skeppskaj 3
shoe *n. com.*	sko (*pl.* skor)
shop *v.*	handla I
shopping mall *n.*	galleria 1
shore/beach *n.*	strand 3
show *v.*	visa I
shrimp sandwich *n.*	räksmörgås
side *n.*	sida 1
sightseeing tour *n.*	rundtur 3
single *adj.*	enkel
sister *n.*	syster (*pl.* systrar)
sit *v.*	sitta IV i-a-u
size *n.*	storlek 2
sleep *v.*	sova IV o-o-o
smaller *adj.*	mindre
smile *v.*	le (ler-låg-lett)
snow *n.*	snö (no plural)

snow v.	snöa I
so adv.	så
sole adj.	enda (enda-enda-enda)
some adj.	någon
someone pro.	någon
someplace adv.	någonstans
something n.	någonting 5
something pro.	något
soon adv.	snart
sort n.	sort 3 or slags 5
sound v.	låta IV å-ä-å
speak v.	tala I
special adj.	speciell
spoon n.	sked 2
square n.	plats 3 or torg 5
stamp n.	frimärke 4
stand v.	stå III
stand n.	kiosk 2
stay n.	vistelse 3
stay v.	stanna I
stop v.	sluta I
store n.	affär 3
straight adv.	rakt
straight ahead adv.	rakt fram
strange adj.	konstig
strange adj.	underlig
street n.	gata 1
stuff v.	stoppa I
sugar n.	socker 5
suggest v.	föreslå III
suit v.	passa I
suitcase n.	väska 1
surf v.	surfa I
sweater n.	tröja 1
Sweden n.	Sverige
Swedish adj.	svensk
Swedish (language) n.	svenska

table *n.*	bord 5
take *v.*	ta (tar-tog-tagit)
talk *v.*	prata I
tax *n.*	skatt 3
taxi *n*	taxi (*pl.* taxi)
telephone *n.*	telefon 3
telephone card *n.*	telefonkort 5
than (with comparisons) *conj.*	än
thank *v.*	tacka I
thanks *n.*	tack
that *pro.*	som
that *conj.*	att
theater *n.*	teater 2
then *adv.*	sedan *or* då
there *adv.* (*dir.*)	dit
there *adv.* (*loc.*)	där
there is/are	det finns
they *pron.*	de
thing *n.*	sak 3
think *v.*	tänka IIb *or* tycka IIb
through *prep.*	genom *or* igenom
ticket *n. com*	biljett 3
time (duration) *n.*	tid 3
time (period) *n.*	gång 3
to *prep.*	till
to (*inf.* particle)	att
today *adv.*	idag
together *adv.*	tillsammans
toilet paper *n.*	toalettpapper 5
too *adv.*	för
toothpaste *n.*	tandkräm 3
tourist information *n.*	turistinformation 3
train *n.*	tåg 5
train card *n.*	tågkort 5
train station *n.*	tågstation 3
travel *v.*	resa IIb
traveler's checks *n.*	resecheckar 2
try *v.*	försöka

try on *v.*	prova I
try out *v.*	prova I
turn *v.*	svänga IIa
unbelievable *adv.*	otroligt
understand *v.*	förstå III
university *n.*	universitet 5
unoccupied *adj.*	ledig
until *conj.*	tills
until *prep.*	förrän
up *adv.* (*dir.*)	upp
up *adv.* (*loc.*)	uppe
upset *adj.*	rubbad
vacation *n.*	semester 2
video machine *n.*	videoapparat 3
vinegar *n.*	vinäger 2
visit *n.*	besök 5
visit (person) *v.*	hälsa på I
waiter *n.*	servitör 3
walk *n.*	promenad 3
walk *v.*	gå V (går-gick-gått)
wander *v.*	vandra I
want *v.*	vilja V (vill-ville-velat)
warm *adj.*	varm
was *v.*	var (*from* vara)
waste *v.*	slösa I
way (custom) *n.*	sätt 5
way (road) *n.*	väg 2
weather *n.*	väder 2
week *n.*	vecka 1
welcome *adj.*	välkommen
welcome *n.*	välkomst 3
welcome (you are welcome) *intrj.*	varsågod
well *intrj.*	nå *or* tjaa
were *v.*	vore (*from* vara)
what *inter.*	vad
where *adv.* (*dir.*)	vart
where *adv.* (*loc.*)	var
which *pro.*	som *or* vilken

white *adj.*	vit
who *pro.*	som
whole *adj.*	hel
wife *n.*	fru 2
wild *adj.*	vild
will *v.*	ska
willingly *adv.*	gärna
winding *adj.*	krokig
wine *n.*	vin (*pl.* viner)
with *prep.*	med
without *conj.*	utan
woman *n.*	kvinna 1
worker *n.*	arbetare (*pl.* -are)
to be worthwhile *v.*	löna sig
would/should *v.*	skulle
write *v.*	skriva IV i-e-i
year *n.*	år 5
yellow *adj.*	gul
yes *intrj.*	ja
yes *intrj.*	jo
you *pro.*	du
young *adj.*	ung
your *pro.*	din

BEGINNER'S SWEDISH
WITH 2 AUDIO CDs
TRACK LIST

DISC ONE

The Swedish Alphabet
Vowels—Front Vowels
Vowels—Back Vowels
Consonants
Letter Combinations
Consonants in Everyday Speech
Lesson 1, Dialogue I
Lesson 1, Dialogue I for repetition
Lesson 1, Dialogue II
Lesson 1, Dialogue II for repetition
Lesson 1, Vocabulary
Lesson 1, Useful Expressions
Lesson 2, Dialogue I
Lesson 2, Dialogue I for repetition
Lesson 2, Dialogue II
Lesson 2, Dialogue II for repetition
Lesson 2, Vocabulary
Lesson 2, Useful Expressions
Lesson 3, Dialogue I
Lesson 3, Dialogue I for repetition
Lesson 3, Dialogue II
Lesson 3, Dialogue II for repetition
Lesson 3, Vocabulary
Lesson 3, Useful Expressions
Lesson 4, Dialogue I
Lesson 4, Dialogue I for repetition

Lesson 4, Dialogue II
Lesson 4, Dialogue II for repetition
Lesson 4, Vocabulary
Lesson 4, Useful Expressions
Cardinal Numbers
Ordinal Numbers
Days of the Week
Months of the Year
Lesson 5, Dialogue I
Lesson 5, Dialogue I for repetition
Lesson 5, Dialogue II
Lesson 5, Dialogue II for repetition
Lesson 5, Vocabulary
Lesson 5, Useful Expressions

DISC TWO

Lesson 6, Dialogue I
Lesson 6, Dialogue I for repetition
Lesson 6, Dialogue II
Lesson 6, Dialogue II for repetition
Lesson 6, Vocabulary
Lesson 6, Useful Expressions
Lesson 7, Dialogue I
Lesson 7, Dialogue I for repetition
Lesson 7, Dialogue II
Lesson 7, Dialogue II for repetition
Lesson 7, Vocabulary
Lesson 7, Useful Expressions
Lesson 8, Dialogue I
Lesson 8, Dialogue I for repetition
Lesson 8, Dialogue II
Lesson 8, Dialogue II for repetition
Lesson 8, Vocabulary
Lesson 8, Useful Expressions
Lesson 9, Dialogue I
Lesson 9, Dialogue I for repetition

Also featuring the work of Scott A. Mellor...

Makes learning words in Swedish
more fun than ever!

- Designed to be the first foreign language dictionary for children ages 5-10.
- 625 total entries
- 500 full-color illustrations
- Featured words are for the people, animals, colors, numbers, and objects children encounter everyday.
- Appendices include everyday expressions, time-related words, and common pronouns.

Full-Color • 625 entries • 112 pages • 8 1/2 x 11 •
ISBN 0-7818-1166-X • $14.95pb • (057)

Sweden

An Illustrated History

By Martina Sprague

With its midnight sun and Gulf Stream climate, Sweden is a land of contradictions. It is home to petroglyphs dating from 9000 BC, thriving high-tech industries, and the ubiquitous design chain Ikea. A comparatively peaceful and economically stable twentieth century secured its reputation as a great place to live, with a solid economy and a generous welfare system. Emigration reversed itself—now more than ten percent of the country's nine million residents were born abroad. When Sweden entered the EU in 1995, its borders became even easier for tourists and immigrants to cross. This short history is ideal for travelers, students, and those with an eye on the new Europe.

234 pages • 5 1/2 x 8 1/2 • **$14.95 paperback** • 0-7818-1114-7 • (097)

A Swedish Kitchen

Recipes and Reminscences

Judith Pierce Rosenberg

A Swedish Kitchen tells the story of an
American woman's 25-year love
affair with the land, people, and
cuisine of this Nordic nation.
Sharing her love of food and
cooking, Judith Pierce Rosenberg
leads readers to markets in search
of wild strawberries and smoked
reindeer, and to cafés for a cup
of strong Swedish coffee and a
kanelbulle (cinnamon bun) or
mazarin (almond tart). Among her
culinary adventures are dinner at
a wilderness lodge, a medieval
banquet, and a Christmas smorgasbord with all the trimmings.
The 80 recipes included highlight traditional Swedish flavors and
ingredients, such as red currants, cloudberries, and cardamom.
Recipes are designed for use in the American kitchen, enabling one
to easily prepare such favorites as *rabarbersoppa* (rhubarb soup),
prinsesstårta (princess cake), and *Janssons frestelse* (Jansson's temptation).

TWO-COLOR • 234 PAGES • 5 ½ X 8 ½
• ISBN 0-7818-1059-0 • $24.95HC • (114)

Prices subject to change without notice. To purchase Hippocrene
Books, contact your local bookstore, visit our website at www.hip-
pocrenebooks.com, call (718) 454-2366, or write to:
HIPPOCRENE BOOKS, 171 Madison Avenue, New York, NY 10016.
Please enclose check or money order, adding $5.00 shipping (UPS)
for the first book, and $.50 for each additional book.